RUFINO TAMAYO

RUFINO TAMAYO

Texts by
OCTAVIO PAZ
JACQUES LASSAIGNE

EDICIONES POLÍGRAFA, S. A.

© 1995 Ediciones Polígrafa, S. A.
Balmes, 54 - Barcelona-7 (Spain)

First edition 1982
Second updated edition 1995

Translated by: KENNETH LYONS
Translation advisor: RICHARD REES

I.S.B.N. 84-343-0795-2
Dep. Legal: B. 39.914-1995 (Printed in Spain)

Printed in Spain by La Polígrafa, S. L.
Parets del Vallès (Barcelona)

CONTENTS

Publisher's Note

A universal creator and yet, at the same time, genuinely Mexican, Rufino Tamayo was not only blessed with immense artistic talent but also possessed a humanist vocation patent both in the subject matter of his oeuvre and in his activities as a collector, a major legacy of which is the Museum of International Contemporary Art which bears his name and which, at the express wish of the master, since 1986 forms part of the national system of museums of the Mexican Instituto Nacional de Bellas Artes.

Until his death in 1991 Rufino Tamayo, an indefatigable experimenter and innovator, remained faithful to his aesthetic ideals which now constitute a major point of reference in Mexican art; by virtue of its variety and extent, his work is the synthesis of a natural and cultural reality in which the younger generations of artists should see the path towards a genuinely autochthonous and original form of expression.

Four years after the death of Rufino Tamayo and shortly after that of his wife, Olga, Ediciones Polígrafa, who in 1982 published a valuable monograph on the artist's work with texts by Octavio Paz and Jacques Lassaigne, has decided to produce a new edition of the book, updated and enriched with reproductions of the last period in the life of the artist.

Barcelona, November 1995

Tamayo, 1981

Tamayo: Geometry and transfiguration

1

There are many ways of approaching a painting: in a straight line where one stands before it and contemplates it face to face, as it were, in an attitude of interrogation, defiance or admiration; obliquely, like somebody exchanging a look of secret understanding with a passer-by; in zigzag fashion, advancing and retreating with strategic movements that recall either those of chessmen or military manoeuvres; measuring and feeling with the eyes, as a greedy guest will eye the fare on a table spread for dinner; or circling round in spirals, like a sparrow hawk before it swoops or a plane waiting to land. The frank way, the conniving way, the reflective way, the hunter's way, the way of the magnetized gaze... For over twenty years now I have been circling round the painting of Rufino Tamayo. I first tried to formulate my impressions in an essay that endeavoured to place him in his most immediate context: modern Mexican painting. Later I wrote a poem, and after that an article of art criticism properly so called: "Tamayo in his painting, his vision of space, the relationship between colour and line, geometry and feeling, volumes and empty surfaces." And now, more cautiously, I am writing these notes: not so much a summing-up as a fresh start.

How can I define my attitude to Tamayo's work? It is a thing of gyration and gravitation; it attracts me and at the same time keeps me at a distance, like a sun. I might also say that it generates a sort of visual appetite: I see his painting as if it were a fruit, incandescent and untouchable. But there is another, more exact word: *fascination.* The picture is there in front of me, hanging on a wall. I look at it and little by little, in slow but inexorable stages, it becomes an opening fan of sensations, a vibration of colours and shapes in an ever-widening series of ripples: a space that is alive, a space that is happy to be space. Later, and just as slowly as before, the colours are furled up again and the picture closes in on itself. There is nothing intellectual about this experience. I am simply describing the act of seeing and the strange though natural fascination that seizes us as we contemplate the daily opening and closing of flowers, fruit, women, the day on the night. Nothing could be further from metaphysical or speculative art than Tamayo's painting. When we look at his pictures we are not witnessing the revelation of a secret; we are sharing in the secret that all revelation amounts to.

2

I have said that Tamayo's painting is not speculative, but perhaps I should have said that it is not ideological. In that essay I wrote in 1950 I pointed out that Tamayo's *historical* importance within the context of Mexican painting consisted in his having called in question, with his exemplary radicalism, the ideological and didactic art of the muralists and their followers. It should be added that Tamayo's true originality — I mean his originality as a painter — does not lie in his critical attitude to the confusion between painting and political literature in which Mexican artists were floundering in those days, but in his critical attitude to objects. In this sense we would be justified in speaking of speculative painting. For it is painting that subjects its object to an inquisition regarding its plastic properties and is an investigation of the relationships between colours, lines and volumes. It is critical painting: the reduction of the object to its essential plastic elements. The object is seen, not as an idea or a representation but as a field of magnetic forces. Each picture is a system of lines and colours rather than a system of signs. The picture may refer to this or that reality, but its plastic meaning is independent.

In Tamayo's first period we find many still lifes, the *Music* mural, the *Homage to Juárez* and other compositions that show a certain affinity, inevitable and natural, with the work of other Mexican artists of that time. But soon he was to give up this style for ever and embark on a very different adventure. Between 1926 and 1938 he painted a great many oils and gouaches, still lifes and landscapes: arches, cubes and terraces that place him, as García Ponce has pointed out, in the line of Cézanne. By going a little further along this road he was to come to Braque. It was not cubist painting but one of the consequences of that movement, one of the roads opened up to art after Cubism. In other canvases of those years we find a freer, more lyrical inspiration that might be described as the exaltation of everyday life through colour, sensuousness rather than eroticism: Matisse. In Tamayo, of course, there is an exasperation and ferocity that we do not find in the work of the great French painter. Other elements in those pictures — and other pictures painted around the same time — brought him close to that other great centre of irradiation, Picasso. Here, however, the lesson he learned was not one of meticulousness or sensuous balance but of passional violence, humour and rage, the revelations of dreams and of eroticism. Not painting as an investigation of the object or as a plastic construction, but painting as an operation that ravaged reality and at the same time was its metamorphosis. At the end of this period Tamayo began to paint a series of violent canvases, sometimes sombre and sometimes exuberantly excited, but always intense and highly concentrated: dogs baying at the moon, birds, horses, lions, lovers in the night, women bathing or dancing, lonely figures gazing up into an enigmatic firmament. Nothing theatrical or dramatic: never was delirium more lucid or more self-controlled. A tragic gaiety. It was in those years that Tamayo discovered the metaphorical powers of colour and form, the gift of language that is painting. The picture became the plastic counterpart of the poetic image. It was not the translation into plastic terms of a verbal poem — a device favoured by several of the Surrealists — but a metaphor already in plastic form, something closer to Miro than to Max Ernst. And so, by a continuous process of assimilation and change, Tamayo turned his painting into an art of transfiguration: that power of the imagination that makes a sun out of a mamey fruit, a half-moon out of a guitar, a stretch of wild countryside out of a woman's body.

I think that the names I have mentioned form a constellation that helps us to situate rather than determine Tamayo's endeavours in the early stages of his career. Which leads me to recall that in the formative period of the Spanish language the word *sino* (fate), which could also be a variant of *signo* (sign), literally meant "constellation". Fate-sign-constellation: Tamayo's fate, and at the same time his signs, as he began his exploration of the world of painting and of that other, more secret world that was his own being, as a man and as a painter. Points of departure for a journey towards himself.

3

Defining an artist by his antecedents is as vain a task as attempting to describe a mature man by the identifying marks of his parents, grandparents or aunts and uncles. The works of other artists — all that comes before, after or simultaneously — can situate the work of an individual, but they cannot define it. Each man's *oeuvre* is a self-sufficient whole that begins and ends in itself. The style of a period is a syntax, a corpus of conscious and unconscious rules with which the artist can say everything that may occur to him, except commonplaces. What counts is not the regularity with which the syntax operates, but the variations: the violations, deviations, exceptions — everything, in short, that makes the work unique. From the very beginning Tamayo's painting has been distinguished from that of all other artists by the predominance of certain elements and the singular way in which he combines them. I will first endeavour to describe these, albeit in a very general way, and then I will try to show how the combination of these elements is equivalent to the transformation of an impersonal, historical syntax into an inimitable language.

Tamayo judges his own work severely and has imposed a strict limitation on himself: painting is, first and foremost, a visual phenomenon. The theme is a mere pretext; what the painter proposes is to set the paint free: it is the forms that speak, not the artist's intentions or ideas. It is the form that emits meanings. Within this aesthetic, which is that of our age, Tamayo's attitude is characterized by its refusal to yield to the easy temptations of literary fantasy. This is not because he regards painting as anti-literary — something it has never been and could never be — but because he insists that the language of painting — its handwriting and its literature — is not verbal but plastic. The ideas and myths, the imaginary passions and figures, the forms we see and those we dream, are realities that the painter must find *within* the painting; something that must spring from the picture, not something inserted in that picture by the artist. Hence

Tamayo's urge to achieve pictorial purity: the canvas on the wall is a two-dimensional surface, closed to the world of words and open to its own reality. Painting is an original language, and one just as rich as music or literature. You can say everything you want to in painting — in painting's own language. Tamayo, of course, would not formulate his proposals in this way. Even in enouncing them thus summarily and verbally, I am afraid of betraying him: his practice of his art is not orthodoxy but orthopraxis.

These preoccupations have led him to a slow, continuous, tenacious pictorial experimentation, an investigation of the secret of textures, colours and their vibrations, the weight and density of materials and impastoes, the laws — and their exceptions — governing the relationships between light and shade, tactile values and volume, line and mass. A passion for what is material, painting that is materialistic in the true sense of the word. Imperceptibly guided by the logic of his investigation, Tamayo passed from a criticism of the object to a criticism of painting itself. An explanation of colour: "as the number of colours we use decreases," he once said to Paul Westheim, "the wealth of possibilities increases. From the pictorial point of view, it is more worthwhile to exhaust the possibilities of a single colour than to use an unlimited variety of pigments." Time and again we have been told that Tamayo is a great colourist; but it should be added that this richness of colour is the result of sobriety. For Baudelaire colour was harmony, an antagonistic and complementary relationship between a hot colour and a cold one. Tamayo takes this quest to extremes, creating harmony within a single colour. In this way he produces a vibration of light in which the resonances, though less far-reaching, are more intense: the furthest point, so taut as to be almost immobile, of a note or tone. Thus limitation becomes abundance, giving us blue and green universes in a pinch of pollen, suns and reddening earths in an atom of yellow, dispersions and conjunctions of hot and cold in an ochre, sharp-painted castles of grey, precipices of white, gulis of violet. But there is nothing gaudy about this abundance. Tamayo's palette is pure; he loves plain colours and, with a kind of instinctive healthiness, shuns any sort of dubious refinement. Delicacy and vitality, sensuousness and energy. If colour is music, there are some pieces by Tamayo that make me think of Bartók, just as the music of Anton von Webern reminds me of Kandinsky.

The same severity characterizes his handling of line and volume. Tamayo draws like a sculptor, and it is a pity that he has given us only a few sculptures. His drawing is that of a sculptor in the vigour and economy of the line, but above all in its essentiality: it indicates the points of convergence, the lines of force that control an anatomy or a form. It is synthetic drawing, with no hint of calligraphy: the true skeleton of painting. Full, compact volumes, living monuments. For the monumental character of a work has nothing to do with its size; it is the product of a relationship between space and the figures inhabiting it. What distinguishes an illustrator from a painter is space: the former sees space as a frame, an abstract limit, while for the latter it is a whole made up of internal relationships, a country ruled by laws of its own. In Tamayo's painting the forms and figures are not *in* space; they *are* space, and they form and conform that space, just as the rocks, hills, riverbeds and groves are not *situated in* the landscape but themselves construct — or, rather, constitute — the landscape. The space Tamayo creates is an animated area made up of weight and movement, forms on the earth, universal obedience to the laws of gravity or to those other, more subtle laws of magnetism. Space here is a field of attraction and repulsion, an arena in which the same forms that move nature engage and disengage, oppose and embrace one another. This is painting as a double of the universe: not its symbol but its projection on the canvas. The picture is not a representation or an ensemble of signs; it is a constellation of forces.

The reflective element is one half of Tamayo; the other half is passion. A contained, introspective passion that never rends its garments or demeans itself with eloquence. And it is this violence, chained or rather unchained upon itself, that at the same time separates him from, and attracts him to, Expressionism in its two main aspects: the German Expressionism of the first quarter of the century and the movement that later came to be known — with a certain latitude of definition — as Abstract Expressionism. The passion that distends forms; the violence of contrasts; the energy that enlivens some of the figures, a dynamism that is resolved in threatening immobility; the brutal exaltation of colour; the fury of some of the brushstrokes and the eroticism of others; trenchant oppositions and unusual alliances: the whole, in short, recalling a line from one of our baroque poets: "beautifully ugly the countenance." This line, indeed, might well be a definition of Expressionism: beauty is neither ideal proportion nor symmetry, but character, energy, breaking — in a word, expression. The marriage of Baroque and Expressionism is more natural than is usually supposed; both are the exaggeration of form, both are styles that underline with red ink. In Tamayo's painting, Baroque and Expressionism have undergone a trial of plastic asceticism; the former has lost its curves and ornaments, the latter its vulgarity and overemphasis. In Tamayo there is no cry of passion, but an almost mineral silence.

I am not proposing definitions; I am venturing approximations. Expressionism, pictorial purity, criticism of the object, a passion for the material, a conception of colour: names, signposts. Reality is something else: Tamayo's pictures. Criticism is not even a translation, though that may be its ideal; it is a guide. And the best criticism is less than that, for it is an invitation to perform the only act that really counts: the act of seeing.

4

Tamayo's great creative period, that of his maturity as a painter, began in New York around 1940. There he spent almost twenty hard but fruitful years. In 1948 he visited Europe for the first time and exhibited in Paris, London, Rome and other European cities. He lived in Paris for some time and returned to Mexico, to settle down permanently, in 1960. His last years in New York, and the early years in Paris, coincided with the appearance and rapid growth of Abstract Expressionism in the United States. In those years, too, important isolated figures were beginning to make their mark in Paris: Fautrier and Dubuffet, not to mention such younger men as Nicolas de Staël, Bacon, Tàpies and that most solitary figure of all, Balthus. The 1940s, in short, saw the emergence of a new group of painters, Tamayo's true contemporaries and, some of them, his equals. It is a generation that has not ceased to astonish us throughout the last twenty-five years, and one whose work is by no means finished yet, although other groups and other trends have naturally appeared since then. Cosmopolitan art, as Baudelaire was the first to observe, is what all modern art has been since it began. This cosmopolitanism has intensified since the Second World War, not only because of the international character of the various styles but also because its leading figures belong to all nations and cultures, not excluding those of the Far East. It is tempting to place Tamayo within this context, as I did before with regard to his predecessors.

If we consider Tamayo's two great Latin-American contemporaries, the Cuban Wifredo Lam and the Chilean Roberto Matta, we will at once see that there are very few points of contact between them and him. But this is not the case if we turn our eyes towards the United States and Europe. What I have called — though with considerable reservations — the Expressionism of Tamayo, has obvious affinities with that of Willem de Kooning and, from another point of view, with the painting of Jean Dubuffet. He is linked to the former, moreover, both by his obsession with the mythical, great-mother-goddess quality of the female body and by the lavish violence of his colour. His affinity with Dubuffet is likewise a dual one: the ferocity of the brushstroke, the fury at and against the human figure, on the one hand and, on the other, his predilection for and preoccupation with textures and their physical properties, whether tactile or visual. They are all three painters of the earth, painters of matter. All three have painted some of the masterpieces of what we might call contemporary pictorial "savagism". All three have humiliated and exalted the human figure. And all three, finally, have created a body of work that stands out from all others and is unmistakable.

The similarities between Tamayo and Dubuffet are as revealing as their differences. I have already spoken of their common love for textures and materials. But Dubuffet's investigation is at once methodical and delirious. It has the rigorousness of reason applied to objects and realities that have always hitherto eluded any quantitative measuring: the general topography of a millimetre of soil, the relief map of a woman's belly, the morphology of beards. Tamayo's attitude is more empirical and instinctive: he does not work with quantities but with qualities. An exhibition by Dubuffet is a demonstration that is at once convincing and overwhelming; on the walls he hangs all the possible variants of a plastic invention. Tamayo looks for unique examples, inventing less and discovering more. The Ariadne's thread of his explorations is not analysis but the logic of correspondences; he slings a bridge between his eyes, his hand and the spirals of glass, wood, skin and the galaxy. Dubuffet uses the razor blade of the syllogism; Tamayo prefers the long-bow of analogy.

Dubuffet represents a radical rationalism, even (or, rather, most of all) when he is painting an apologia of irrationalism and *art brut*. He is so intelligent that he paints with the totalitarian logic of a madman, but lucidity, which is at once his gift and his punishment, never really abandons him: for madmen do have moments when they know that they are mad and know, too, that they cannot cease to be mad, whereas Dubuffet knows that he is not mad and that he never will be. His childish paintings are the impressive work of a child who is a thousand years old, a visionary, demoniac child who knows and has not forgotten the syntaxes of all styles. Dubuffet's creativeness is critical, his ferocity mental. His work is not a celebration of reality. His cannibalism, socially and morally justified, would horrify real cannibals; it is not a ritual, but the macabre game of irony and despair. Not a communion, but a glutton on an operating table. Deliriums of reason. A world which, not only by its violence but also because of its systematic character, evokes the name of Sade rather than that of Goya.

Dubuffet's genius is encyclopedic; Tamayo's, though no less rich, is less vast. His pictures, too, are peopled with monsters; his brush flays human beings just as cruelly. For this artist, who is sometimes so gay and tender, also knows how to be cruel: humour occupies a central position in his work. But the roots of his cruelty are neither irony nor system, but satire and the sense of the grotesque. A love for monsters, phenomena and freaks is at once an Indian and a Spanish heritage. Pre-Columbian art abounds in deformed creatures, and the same can be said of the golden age of Spanish painting. Montezuma had his hunchbacks, Philip IV his zany buffoons and dwarfs. Tamayo's painting is rich in monstrous characters, sordid or farcical: the glutton, the laughing-man, the society lady, the maniac, the idiot and other ridiculous creatures. Among his terrible images there is one that has all the value of an emblem without losing that other, more immediate value of being an everyday reality: the bone, the heap of bones that is all we are. Bones of dogs, a bone moon, bone bread, man's bones, a bone landscape: a charnel planet. This obsession with bones begins by being satirical but later becomes a cosmic image. Tamayo's ferocity is not intellectual; it is satire and ritual, earthy mockery and magic ceremony. His madmen are pathetic and grotesque, but not despicable; his monsters are vital creatures, freaks or abortions of nature, but not metaphysical caricatures. In his distortions of the human figure we may read the signs, the handwriting, of the havoc and victories of passion, of time and of the inhuman forces of money and machines. His world is the physical world. Rain, blood, muscles, semen, sun, drought, stone, bread, vagina, laughter, hunger: all of them words which, for Tamayo, have not only meaning but also savour, smell, taste, weight, colour.

Tamayo's oppositions to, and similarities with, de Kooning are of a different kind. For Dubuffet the danger is the system; for Tamayo it is aestheticism; for Willem de Kooning, the gesture. In de Kooning there is a vital and absolutely unsystematical lavishness that moves us and wins us over. His sensuousness is violent, but its violence represents a desire to attain harmony with the forces of life. The other face of harmony is discord. And these two words form the axis of his work. All of this brings him close to Tamayo, a painter who also obeys the heart and its impulses. In the New York painter's work Dore Ashton finds two elements: a passional impulse, alternatively demoniac and orgiastic, and a tendency to the Baroque. The female body, the centre of his art even in his non-figurative compositions, epitomizes the duality of these elements. The paradox of eroticism: in the act of love we possess the body of a woman as a whole broken up into fragments; simultaneously, each fragment — an eye, a piece of a cheek, an ear lobe, the gleam of a thigh, the shadow of the hair falling on a shoulder, the lips — alludes to the other fragments and, in a way, contains the whole. The bodies are the theatre in which the show we see is, in fact, the interplay of the universal correspondence, the relationship — unceasingly dissolved and remade — between unity and plurality. If it is eroticism that unites these two artists, it is the Baroque that separates them. I have already described the character of the Baroque in Tamayo, and the severe limitations it imposes on him. This severity is not present in de Kooning. In de Kooning there is overflowing; in Tamayo, concentration. They are two different versions of the orgiastic: the Flemish kermesse and the Mexican fiesta.

The passional and demoniac element in Tamayo corresponds to what I have called *transfiguration,* the analogical imagination. For Tamayo the world is still a system of summonses and responses, man is still part of the earth — *is,* in fact, the earth. Tamayo's attitude is more *ancient:* it is, I mean, closer to the origins. It is one of the privileges, offsetting so many disadvantages, of having been born in an underdeveloped country.

In de Kooning we find romantic vitalism: man is alone in the world. Tamayo, on the contrary, represents naturalism: a vision of the unity between the world and man. De Kooning has said: "When I think of painting today, I find myself always thinking of that part which is connected with the Renaissance. It is the vulgarity and fleshy part of it which seems to make it particularly Western." There could hardly be anything less "fleshy" than Tamayo's painting: the same asceticism that prevents him from falling into the baroque temptation of the curve is what saves him from hurling himself into the softness of the flesh. As is the case with all great artists, death is a constant presence in Tamayo's painting. It is a severe and introspective presence: not the vertigo of the fall, not the pomp and splendour of the putrefaction of Baroque, but the geometry of bones, their whiteness, their hardness and the infinitesimally fine dust they become.

5

My purpose in the foregoing notes was to describe Tamayo's attitude to painting and the place his own painting occupies in the world of contemporary art, as also the relationship between the painter and his work, and that between the latter and the work of other painters. For there is another relationship that is no less decisive: Tamayo and Mexico.

All the critics have remarked on the importance of popular art in Tamayo's work. This term — "popular art" — what does it mean? Is it traditional art or art of the people? Pop art, for instance, is popular but not traditional. It does not carry on a tradition, but endeavours, sometimes successfully, to use popular elements in order to create works that are new and explosive, which is quite the opposite of a tradition. True popular art, on the contrary, is always traditional; it is a manner, a style, that is perpetuated by repetition and permits only slight variations. There are no aesthetic revolutions in the world of popular art. Besides, the repetition and variations are anonymous — or, rather, impersonal and collective. The history of art has always, quite rightly, stressed the importance of styles. But if it is true that the notions of art and style are inseparable, it is no less so that works of art are violations, exceptions or exaggerations of artistic styles. Style, whether baroque or impressionist, is a repertoire of plastic terms, a syntax that becomes meaningful only when a unique work violates the common style. What matters is the singular exception, the unrepeatable work. In this sense popular art, since it constitutes a traditional style without interruptions or creative changes, is not really *art* in any strict meaning of that word. Besides, it has never had any ambition to be regarded as art: it is simply an extension of ordinary utensils and ornaments, aspiring only to blend into man's everyday existence. Its place is in the sphere of festivity, ceremony and work: it is social life crystallized into a magic object. And I say *magic* because it seems highly probable that the origins of popular art are to be sought in the magic that is the concomitant of all religions and beliefs: offering, talisman, relic, fertility rattle, clay figure, family fetiche. If we are to seek the relationship between Tamayo and popular art, therefore, it must be at the deepest level: not in the forms but in the beliefs that give them life.

I do not say that Tamayo has been insensible to the charm of popular plastic inventions; I am merely pointing out that their function is neither exclusively nor even principally aesthetic. They do not appear in his pictures on account of their beauty, though they may be beautiful, nor yet as an expression of some unbridled nationalistic or populist feeling. Their meaning is quite different: they are transmitting channels that link Tamayo with the world of his childhood. Their importance is affective and existential: the artist is the man who has not completely buried his childhood. Apart from this psychic function, and on a still deeper level, these popular forms may be likened to irrigation ditches, through which run the ancestral sap, the original beliefs, the unconscious (but not incoherent) thought that animates the world of magic. Magic, says Cassirer, affirms the brotherhood of all living beings because it is based on the belief in a universal energy or fluid. There are two consequences of magical thought: metamorphosis and analogy. Metamorphosis means that all forms and their changes are transmutations of the original fluid; analogy means that everything corresponds to everything else if the transformations of beings and things are governed by a single principle. Irrigation, circulation of the essential breath: one sole energy goes through everything, from insect to man, from man to spectre, from spectre to plant, from plant to star. If magic is the animation of the universe, popular art is its survival: in its fragile, enchanting forms it holds the secret of metamorphosis. It is because Tamayo has drunk from this spring that he knows the secret. Not with his head but in the only way we moderns can know it: with his eyes and his hands, with his body and with the unconscious logic of what we so inaccurately call instinct.

Tamayo's relationship with pre-Columbian art does not show itself in the sphere of beliefs but on the conscious level of aesthetics. Before describing this relationship, however, there are some misunderstandings that must be cleared up. I refer to the frequent confusion of the artist's nationality and that of his art. It is not difficult to see, at first sight, the "Mexican-ness" of Tamayo's painting; and it is equally easy, if we reflect a little, to perceive that this is a feature that defines his art only very superficially. No work, in any case, can be defined by its nationality, and still less so by that of its creator. When we say that Cervantes is Spanish and Racine French, we have said little or nothing about Cervantes or Racine. So let us forget Tamayo's nationality and consider instead the circumstances determining his encounter with the ancient art of Mexico. The first thing that should be emphasized is the distance that separates us from the Meso-American world. The Spanish conquest was something more than a conquest; it meant the destruction by violence of the whole Meso-American civilization and the beginning of a different society. Between the pre-Hispanic past and ourselves there is no continuity like that which exists between the China of the Han dynasty and that of today, or between Japan as it was under Heian-Kio and the industrial giant we know now. We must therefore define, albeit in very broad outline, our peculiar position vis-à-vis the Meso-American past.

The reconquest of pre-Hispanic art was an undertaking that would have been impossible had it not been for two determinant factors: the Mexican Revolution and the cosmopolitan aesthetic appreciation of the Western World. About the former so much has been written that I need mention only what seems to me essential. Thanks to the revolutionary movement our country has felt itself to be what it is, seen itself for what it is: a hybrid country, closer to its Indian roots than to the European in the racial aspect, but not so as far as culture and political institutions are concerned. This discovery of ourselves led us to regard with equally impassioned interest the remains of the ancient civilization and its survival in popular beliefs and customs. That is why modern Mexico has made such great efforts to recover this magnificent past. The roots of Mexico as it is today are Indian, and there are many cultural, social and psychic survivals from the pre-Hispanic societies. Indeed, it is inexact to speak of them as survivals, for they should more properly be called mental and social structures. And it is these structures, half-buried, that inform and conform our myths, our aesthetics, our ethics and our politics. As a *civilization,* however, the Indian world is dead. We venerate the relics of Meso-America and collect them in our museums, but we have not attempted — nor would it be possible — to resuscitate the victim. It is at this point that the other factor comes into play: the European vision of civilizations and traditions other than those of Greece and Rome.

This discovery of other societies and cultures is quite a recent one. It began at almost the same time as the imperialistic expansion of some European countries, and the first testimonies we have of it are the accounts, chronicles and descriptions written by Portuguese or Spanish explorers and conquistadores. Anthropology, in fact, was born with writers like Sahagún and Motolinia. It was the other face of discovery and conquest: an affective and intellectual *conversion* which, in revealing the humaneness and wisdom of non-European societies, at the same time revealed the remorse and horror that were felt by some consciences at the destruction of peoples and civilizations. Then the eighteenth century, with its curiosity and respect for Chinese civilization and its exaltation of the noble savage, went a step further and opened people's minds to a less ethnocentric concept of the human species. And so, little by little, as though in a critical counterpoint to the atrocities committed in Asia, Africa and America, the European vision of other peoples changed. But the ultimate disaster was that at the very time when anthropology was being established as a science, the decline of the last primitive societies began. And finally, in our own century, at the moment of its victory and with all other civilizations destroyed or petrified, the Western World discovered itself in racial persecutions, imperialism, war and totalitarianism. It is only in our time that the civilization of historical consciousness, that great European invention, has discovered the self-destroying forces that inhabit it. The twentieth century shows us that our place in history is not so very different from that of the Assyrians of Sargon II, the Mongols of Genghis Khan or the Aztecs of Itzcoatl.

The change in the European aesthetic vision was even slower in coming. Though Dürer did not hide his admiration for Mixtecan gold and silver work, it was not until the nineteenth century that this isolated opinion was adopted as an aesthetic doctrine. The German Romantics discovered Sanskrit literature and Gothic art; their followers all over Europe developed an interest in the world of Islam and the civilizations of the Far East; and finally, at the beginning of the present century, the arts of Africa, America and Oceania appeared on the aesthetic horizon. Without the modern artists of the West, who took possession of all that immense body of styles and visions of reality and transformed it into living, contemporary works of art, the Mexicans of today would never have been able to understand and love pre-Columbian art. Mexican artistic nationalism stems directly both from the change in social consciousness brought about by the Mexican Revolution and from the change in artistic consciousness that came with European aesthetic cosmopolitanism.

This digression has, I hope, helped the reader to see more clearly the nature of the confusion between nationalism and the pre-Columbian past. In the first place, pre-Columbian art cannot be said to be Mexican at all, strictly speaking; Mexico did not even exist when it was created, nor were its creators even aware of the modern political concept that we call a nation. In the second place, and even more strictly speaking, it is a debatable point whether the arts have any nationality at all. What they do have is *style;* but of what nationality is Gothic art, for instance? And even if they had a nationality, what significance would it have? There is no national copyright in art. The great contemporary critic of medieval French art is called Panofsky, while Berenson was the greatest authority on Italian painting of the Renaissance. The best studies of Lope de Vega are probably those of Vossler. And the great tradition of Spanish painting was not carried on by the mediocre Spanish painters of the nineteenth century, but by Manet. No, the understanding of pre-Columbian art is not an inherited privilege of the Mexicans. It is the result of an act of love and reflection, as in the case of the German critic Paul Westheim, or of an act of creation, as in that of the English sculptor Henry Moore. In art there can be no inheritances: there are discoveries, conquests, affinities, abductions, re-creations that are really creations. Tamayo is no exception. It was modern aesthetics that opened his eyes and made him see the modernity of pre-Hispanic sculpture. Later, with the violence and simplicity of all creative artists, he made those forms his own and transformed them. I mean that he took them as his starting-point for painting new and original forms. It is true that popular art had already fertilized his imagination and prepared it to accept and assimilate the art of ancient Mexico. But without modern aesthetics that initial impulse would have been dissipated or would have degenerated into mere folklore and decoration.

If we consider the two poles that define Tamayo's painting — plastic rigorousness and the imagination that transfigures the object — we will at once see that his encounter with pre-Columbian art was a truly momentous one. I will begin with the first: the purely plastic relationship. The immediate and surprising qualities of pre-Columbian sculpture are the strict geometry of its conception, the solidity of its volumes and its admirable fidelity to its material. These were the qualities that impressed modern artists and critics from the start. And Tamayo's attitude follows the same reasoning: like modern painting, Meso-American sculpture is principally a logic of forms, lines and volumes. And this plastic logic, unlike that of Graeco-Roman or renaissance art, is not based on the imitation of the proportions of the human figure but on a radically different conception of space, a conception which in the eyes of the Meso-Americans was religious, whereas for us it is intellectual. In either case it is a *non-human* vision of space and of the world. Modern thought holds that man is no longer the centre of the universe or the measure of all things. This idea is not far removed from the vision the ancient Mexicans had of man and the cosmos. There are artistic correspondences to these contradictory conceptions: in the renaissance tradition the human figure is so absolutely central that there have even been attempts to subject the very landscape to its sway (the humanization of the countryside in sixteenth- and seventeenth-century poetry, for instance, or the subjectivism of the Romantics); in pre-Columbian and modern art, on the contrary, that same human figure is subjected to the geometry of a non-human space. In the first case we have the cosmos as a reflection of man; in the second, man as a symbol of the cosmos. On the one hand, humanism and realistic illusionism; on the other, abstraction and a symbolic vision of reality. The *symbolism* of ancient art becomes *transfiguration* in Tamayo's painting. In the Meso-American tradition he discovered something more than a logic and a grammar of forms; it showed him, in even livelier fashion than Klee or the Surrealists, that the plastic object is a high-frequency transmitter that sends out a plurality of meanings and images. Thus the lesson of pre-Hispanic art is a double one: firstly, it teaches fidelity to the material and the form (for an Aztec, a stone sculpture is sculpted stone), then that this sculpted stone is a metaphor of stone — geometry and transfiguration.

This leads me to wonder whether Tamayo did not know all that already. His encounter with pre-Columbian art was not so much a discovery as a confirmation. Perhaps the true name of creation is *recognition.*

6

In the course of these reflections I have used two words repeatedly: tradition and criticism. I have frequently pointed out — and I am not alone in this — that criticism is the substance, the very life-blood, of the modern tradition. Criticism conceived as an instrument of creation, not simply as judgment or analysis. That is why every new work takes a polemical attitude to its predecessors. Our tradition is a living thing, perpetuated by means of the successive negations and breaks that it engenders. In our eyes the only dead art is art that is not worthy of the supreme homage of creative negation. The difference from the past is significant: the artists of past ages imitated the masterpieces of their predecessor. Within this tradition that is constantly in crisis (and is now approaching its end) it is possible to make yet another distinction: there are artists — such as Mallarmé or Duchamp — who turn criticism into an absolute and, to some extent, make their negation a creation; and there are others — Yeats, Matisse — who use criticism as a springboard that helps to propel them to other lands, other affirmations. The former bring their language (poetry, music, painting) to a crisis; they confront language and criticism without any appeal to silence. The latter use that same silence as a recourse of language. It is what I have called, within the modern tradition of breaking, the No and Yes families. Tamayo belongs to the second of these.

He is a painter of painting, not of the metaphysics or criticism of painting. He is the absolute opposite of such a painter as Mondrian or, to speak of his contemporaries, Barnett Newman. He is more akin to painters like Braque or Bonnard. Reality for Tamayo is corporal, visual. Yes, the world exists: we are told so by his reds and purples, the iridescence of his greys, the smudginess of charcoal; we hear it from the smooth surface of this stone, the knots in the wood, the coldness of the water snake; the triangle and the octagon, the dog and the beetle, all proclaim it. Sensations tell us the same. The relationships between the sensations and the structures or forms they create as they entwine and disengage are what we call painting. Painting is the translation of the world into tangible terms, and translating the world into painting means perpetuating it, prolonging it. This is the origin of Tamayo's rigorous attitude to painting. This attitude is not so much an aesthetic as a profession of faith: painting for him is a way of *touching* reality. It does not give us the sensation of reality: it confronts us with the reality of sensations. And the most immediate and direct of these are colours, forms, touch. A material world which, without losing its materiality, is also a mental world: those colours are painted colours. The whole of Tamayo's critical investigation tends to save painting, to preserve its purity and perpetuate its mission as a translator of the world. Tamayo is against literature quite as much as he is against abstraction, against the geometry that turns it into a skeleton and against the realism that demeans it to the level of a lying illusion.

The translation of the world into tangible terms is a transmutation. A transmutation in painting is a different process from that of verbal language: in a text we read signs (words and letters), whereas in a painting we see tangible forms (colours, lines). But the painter must put those forms in order. And the order he imposes on them is always symbolic, for otherwise painting would not be language. In Tamayo's case this symbolism is not abstract: his world, as André Breton pointed out, is everyday life. This observation would be of no interest if Breton himself had not gone on to say that Tamayo's art consisted in inserting everyday life into the sphere of poetry and ritual. That is to say, an art of transfiguration. That web of pictorial sensations which is a painting by Tamayo is likewise a metaphor. And what does that metaphor tell us? The world exists, life is life, death is death: *everything is.* And this statement, which does not exclude either unhappiness or chance, is an act of the imagination rather than of the will or the understanding. The world exists thanks to the imagination, which, in transfiguring it, reveals it to us.

7

If I could express with a single word what it is that distinguishes Tamayo from other painters of our age, I would say, without a moment's hesitation: *sun.* For the sun is in all his pictures, whether we see it or not; night itself for Tamayo is simply the sun carbonized.

Octavio Paz (1982)

Rufino Tamayo at the Museo de Antropología de México. Photo: Juan Guzmán.

Training and choice

Rufino Tamayo was born in 1899 in the city of Oaxaca, capital of the province of the same name in that southwestern region of Mexico where the Zapotecs, a race whose features Tamayo has clearly inherited, built the ancient cities of Monte Albán and Mitla. On the death of his parents he left Oaxaca and went to live in Mexico City with an aunt who brought him up to help her in her fruit shop. He also attended school — the aunt being of the opinion that he should attend commercial courses that would give him a proper business training. But her nephew, even at that early age, had a mind of his own in such matters and enrolled secretly in evening classes in drawing.

By 1917 his vocation was settled and he began to attend the courses at the San Carlos Academy of Fine Arts. He did not stay there very long, soon becoming dissatisfied with the teaching offered there. What he did learn, though, he assimilated properly and never forgot. In 1921 he got a job in the Department of Ethnographic Drawings at the National Archaeological Museum. His work consisted principally in making available to craftsmen from all over the country the original models of the Museum's pre-Columbian drawings. The purpose was to give some semblance of authenticity to all the objects they made for sale to the international tourist trade, which was becoming more and more important.

This work, which he obtained thanks to the disinterested and enlightened protection of José Vasconcelos, Minister for Education during the presidency of Álvaro Obregón, was to bring him into direct contact with objects selected from among those regarded as most characteristic of the ancient art of Mexico — objects which he would certainly never have been able to study so systematically if he had not been on the Museum staff. This experience constituted for Tamayo a sort of revelation that was to have a decisive influence on the techniques he later invented and put into practice, but even more so on his artistic sensibility. Of this we have evidence in an important work dated in 1931, *Nude in Grey.* This monumentally-proportioned seated figure is like some dark idol rearing its heavy mass against a red background; it is a magic character, full of mystery, and yet it is absolutely feminine. It is like a

Tamayo, 1926. Photo: Manuel Álvarez Bravo.

prefiguration of the painter's whole *oeuvre*, of which this early example gives a strange impression of suspended animation, of an event taking shape in silence and inspiring astonishment or fear. This work is also of an initiatory character, with insistent mutations that reveal its enduring assimilation to a past tradition of such immensity that it has not yet been fully explored. By 1926 Tamayo had done enough works in this line to hold an exhibition in some almost anonymous premises in Mexico City — which at that time did not yet possess a single art gallery.

But these early creations — which have taken a long time to be recognized as the important works they are — were far from satisfying Tamayo, who wanted to see for himself the different forms taken by modern art all over the world. He needed to touch, to see with his own eyes, all that was as yet only a feeling. And so he left for New York, where he was to stay for two years: two years of investigation, discoveries, work and encounters with different works of art and artists. I believe we must attribute to fate rather than mere chance the fact that Tamayo so quickly discovered the work of Rouault, which impressed him so deeply as representing a totally committed adventure quite different from that of any other artist. Another discovery that he made at a very early stage was the sculpture of Brancusi. Two very important exhibitions of modern painting — *From Ingres to Picasso* and *French Art of the Last 50 Years* — served as his introduction to the works of the Impressionists, the Fauvists and the Cubists. It was also during this time in 1928 that Tamayo first came into contact with Matisse at a large showing of his works at the Brooklyn Museum.

During this period in New York he continued his own work in the light of all his investigations and contacts he had made with painters and critics. New York represented to Tamayo a sort of ideal half-way point between his original sources in Mexico and the most decisive trends in European painting: a neutral ground on which opposing extremes could be reconciled, a place where there was nothing as yet to distract him from a meditation wholly centred on his art. And, indeed, the great innovations which impressed him so much, without influencing him directly, were simply a means — or perhaps I should say a stimulus — of going more deeply into that colourful language he had built up for himself already in Mexico, the real origins of which I would be inclined to place even further back in time. A language in which, despite Tamayo's early stylistic investigations, absolute priority was very soon given to colour, defined as a dominant characteristic which could give all the meaning and which was to be the most typical feature of his work for the rest of his life.

On his return to Mexico in 1928, Tamayo was appointed to a post as a teacher of painting at the National School of Fine Arts, of which Diego Rivera was then Principal. But this was to be a short-lived experience. For Tamayo right from the start adopted a position of absolute independence with regard to the great renaissance of Mexican mural painting which had followed the triumph of the 1910 Revolution and had produced some glorious ensembles of decorations exalting the history of the country, its races, its civilizations and its successive social transformations. He could afford his independent stance and his experience in New York gave him the confidence. "Too young," Tamayo later wrote, "to have been able to influence this Mexican pictorial movement when it first began, I disapproved of the direction my predecessors had given it. Whatever the qualities revealed by the painting of the initial period, the painters' obsession with practising not so much painting as *Mexican* painting (though, in fact, only apparently so) led them to neglect the real plastic problems and to fall into the trap of the picturesque. Seeing what had happened, and even though I was myself convinced that our painting should be Mexican *in its essence* (but without on that account forgetting the technical aspects, which had been neglected), I reacted very strongly against the established conventions and started a movement that aimed at restoring to our painting its purest qualities."

The three great Mexican painters of that time, Diego Rivera, José Clemente Orozco and David Alfaro Siqueiros, represent one of the most important moments in the history of Latin American art. Their mural work is undoubtedly intended to be above all political and sociological,

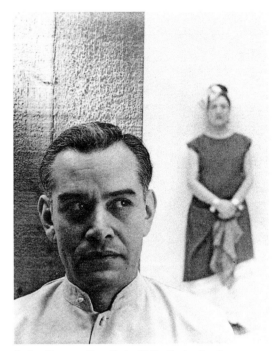
Rufino Tamayo, New York, 1941. Photo: Rawlings.

Tamayo at a party in Xochimilco.

Tamayo, 1935.

which takes nothing away from its expressive plastic grandeur, but which marks its time and its limitations — limitations by which Tamayo certainly did not intend to be fettered. The Mexican Revolution was a true national movement of the people, a struggle against the great landowners, descendants of the Spanish invaders. This revolt by the peasants was followed by a reaction of sympathy on the part of the intellectuals and artists, who wanted to revive the ancient civilizations of Mexico and to recover in its entirety its multiplicity of cultures and races, in order to build the new Mexico in their image.

For the first time in the country's history there was a progressive government which encouraged the artistic expression of a new movement; a government which wanted to restore to the people their consciousness of the old cultural traditions of their country and of their new and permanent "Mexican-ness". Vast mural paintings presenting scenes in the life of the people were to prove highly efficacious as the new media of communication. The exaltation of freedom was to find its reason, first in themes taken from folklore and from the colonial epic, then in episodes of contemporary history.

In producing this great work the three famous muralists never resorted to the language of academicism, as was so often the case in Europe with other neorealistic exaltations of nationalism. Rivera, indeed, during his European period had taken part in the experiments of the Cubists. A recent exhibition in Paris, moreover, has shown the mistakes and weaknesses of these so-called returns to order and realism. It would be quite unjust, however, to confuse Mexican mural painting with the sorry avatars of the various modern realisms, socialist or not socialist. Seen from our present distance, indeed, the famous conflict between Tamayo and his immediate predecessors seems to have been an affair of differences of intensity more than anything else. Their works, though they are certainly different, are both successive in time and complementary (Tamayo, too, is a great muralist). In a recent interview with the Argentinean journalist Alfredo Andrés, Tamayo defined his position in the following terms: "I do not believe in either Mexican or

Latin American painting. I can only conceive of painting in its most universal sense. The increasing importance of the mass media, above all since the Second World War, has done away with everything that could be localistic... I have always been opposed to that sort of pseudo-Mexican art. The most one can say is that there is a kind of common stamp, since all of us do belong to a certain place and to a certain moment in time. But art is universal. If one has authentic roots, there is no need to look for anything: that stamp that identifies us will appear of its own accord. My position has brought me a lot of problems in my country; sometimes I have been regarded as a sort of black sheep of painting. The others were painting Indians and socio-political events, but concerning themselves exclusively with external aspects, without ever going to the heart of things. And anybody who didn't conform to that idea of painting was lost. That was why I decided to go to New York, and it was in that city that my conception of a universalistic art was, in fact, confirmed."

Rufino Tamayo in Manila (Philippines).

On being asked to define his relationships with his predecessors, Tamayo said: "Their ambition was to create a national art, but they were using the techniques of the Renaissance. They painted frescoes to glorify the bravery of the peasants during the Mexican Revolution... Personally, what interests me most is easel painting, which I see as a sort of laboratory for constant experimenting. That would be impossible with mural painting, for it is always subordinated to architecture. With the easel, on the contrary, one is confronted with two dimensions, which proves the absurdity of those who say that easel painting is dead. It is not dead for the simple reason that it performs a specific function: expression in two dimensions... In much the same fashion we might say that Kinetic Art, though it is an extremely interesting contribution to art in general, will never take the place of painting."

In the same interview Tamayo went on to say: "My main concern, really, is to resolve the picture with its own elements: to define its balance, with that mysterious sort of mathematics which, even when it is applied intuitively, makes it possible to turn a picture upside down without any loss of significance, quite independently of the subject — for the subject

Rufino Tamayo with Henry Moore
at Xochicalco, Morelos.

Tamayo at Xochicalco, Morelos.

doesn't really matter. But what interests me most of all is man and the way he faces the problems that surround him. Art must belong to its time: it should not be concerned with memories but with what is happening now. And the artist is an antenna. He cannot be passive or content merely to dream. Art is fundamentally a message, a means of communication; it involves a message."

For the catalogue of his Paris exhibition Rufino Tamayo has set forth, in eight precise paragraphs, the way in which he practises painting, that vocation which has the almost craftsmanlike virtues of simplicity.

How I paint:

1. As a general rule, I work directly on the canvas, without making any preparatory sketches, in an immediate transposition of the real forms that serve as the picture's motif.

2. I begin to work by drawing the general structure of the picture, and on that structure I build with paint.

3. I have never worked in artificial light, because I consider that only natural light gives the colours their precise tonal values.

4. Although I have painted on all sorts of surfaces, I think that canvas, thanks to its extraordinary texture, is the one that offers most possibilities for handling pictorial material.

5. My palette is very limited, as limited as possible, for I think that the secret of colour consists not in the use of all the colours in existence but, on the contrary, in the proper handling of just a few, from which one may extract all the possibilities of tone.

6. In my painting I make use of all sorts of working tools, for each one produces a different texture. In this way one obtains a greater wealth of pictorial material.

Rufino Tamayo in a market, Oaxaca.

Olga and Tamayo in Cuernavaca.

7. I use canvases that have been already sized, and of the best quality possible. I think they are really good; besides, one can choose them according to the texture and degree of absorbency one wishes. As far as colours are concerned, since the ready-made colours to be found in the shops frequently lack the proper consistency, I usually prepare my own according to my needs.

8. I always work on one canvas at a time until it is finished. But since every new work entails experiments with new textures, the canvases often have to be left to dry before the fresh layers of pigments can be superimposed. And then I sometimes do try to paint two pictures at the same time, so as not to interrupt my working rhythm.

A different muralism

Although Tamayo's work very soon revealed a break with, or at any rate a divergence from, the usual practice of Mexican muralism, he nevertheless played his part — and a far from negligible one — in the expression of social, political and perhaps even more transcendental ideas through the medium of mural painting. Certainly he can by no means be regarded as an apolitical figure. On one occasion he was chosen as one of the delegates of the Mexican League of Revolutionary Painters and Artists to represent that organization at an important conference to be held in New York. He has never gone out of his way to avoid political discussions and has taken a normal part in the sort of polemics that are always apt to break out in Mexico. As examples of this I might mention the many exchanges of views — not always particularly affable — that he had with Siqueiros in the years 1947, 1950, 1954 and 1957.

Mural for the United Nations, New York.

Apart from all this, however, Tamayo himself has painted many mural works in his day, not only in Mexico but also in the United States and in France. I would say in this respect, moreover, that he has not confined himself to expressing social protest related to events in Mexico's past of contemporary history, but has broadened the range of his convictions to include the exaltation of universal myths, of concepts which to him seem essential for all mankind — and which, moreover, were already among the themes of his easel painting. Thus, in the Palace of Fine Arts of Mexico he rendered the theme of the nations's birth with all the required didactic content; but the truth is that his style was better adapted to more general themes, as we may see in *Man,* in the Dallas Museum of Fine Arts, or *Nature and the Artist,* in the library of Smith College, Northampton; and when he was asked for a subject sufficiently important to grace the UNESCO headquarters in Paris, he could think of nothing more suitable than *Prometheus Bringing Fire to Mankind.*

After his first mural painting, which was commissioned in 1933 for the Conservatorio Nacional de Música de México and, naturally, dealt with a musical theme, Tamayo painted almost a score of large-scale compositions of this type. Right from the start he showed a preference for existential or cosmic themes, but when he was given a commission to evoke the Revolution for the Museo Nacional de Antropología de

In his Paris studio, 1957.

Tamayo with the ex-President of Mexico, Miguel Alemán.

México, or to exalt Mexico's nationhood for the Palacio de Bellas Artes, he was perfectly capable of dealing with such subjects. Apart from these two exceptions, however, his mural work is wholly given up to themes which, independently of whether they have been suggested by others or not, he accepts because they relate to more abstract notions or to myths that affect him personally. Thus, for instance, the pair of complementary panels that he painted for Smith College, Northampton — *Nature and the Artist: The Work of Art and the Observer* — symbolically unite two successive and complementary moments of the Creation. In 1956 he painted a vast allegorical picture with geometrical forms for the Bank of the Southwest in Houston, a homage to America, represented as a recumbent figure in the lower part of the composition. According to what he wrote to Emily Ganauer, Tamayo wanted "this figure to transmit, through its heroic proportions, the ideal of abundance that constitutes this continent's principal characteristic." And this abundance is likewise represented by the fish, a symbol of the riches of the sea surrounding the main symbolic figure, by a plant, which symbolizes the riches of the earth, by an oil gusher and by a bubbling spring pouring forth its subterranean wealth of water. In the upper part of the composition there are two entwined figures, signifying the fusion of races which have gone to make up America, and whose cultural contributions have so enriched the continent's spirit. The figure on the left, next to the cross, is that of the white race, while the darker figure on the right is that of the Amerindian race, whose contribution is represented by Quetzalcoatl, the plumed serpent of the pre-Columbian culture.

This symbolism, as a matter of fact, is not so very different from that adopted at an earlier date by Orozco, Rivera and Siqueiros. But this submission to a manner proposed by others was not to last very long or to be repeated very often. In such commissions as he accepted from then on, Tamayo's forms were progressively stripped of all inessentials and every work, however vast its scale, was painted in accordance with the essentially pictorial values that the painter derived from his experiments with easel painting. Thus, the two great mural compositions that he did on the theme of Prometheus, first in 1957 for the library

a, b and c. Three moments during the visit paid by
Prince Takamatzu (the Emperor's brother) and his
wife to the opening of the Tamayo exhibition at the
Museum of Modern Art, Tokyo, 1963.

d. A present to Tamayo from the Mainichi
Newspaper, 1963.

e. In Tokyo with the editors of the Mainichi
Newspaper, 1963.

Ekeley, Oslo. 17th February 1959.

Olga and Tamayo, 1975.

of the University of Puerto Rico and then in 1958 for the UNESCO headquarters in Paris, are like some enormous conflagration resulting from the combustion of all the reds imaginable, those reds with which he had experimented in his more personal pictures.

His evocation of *Energy,* painted in 1969 for the "Club de los Industriales de México", is a dazzling explosion of curvilinear forms that compose the most beautiful abstract painting he has ever done. Then, in his *Man Facing the Heavens,* in the Hotel Camino Real in Mexico, he returns to the theme of the great composition of an executed man, which he painted for the Dallas Museum in 1952, and in which we see an immensely tall figure, with very geometrical lines, advancing majestically over the earth, transfixed by rays that shoot forth from the stars and join it to the infinite. It is as though the comet that dominates the composition were the projection of man himself dominating the universe which he is exploring by dint of a supreme effort and tension. In the more recent of these works (the one painted in 1970) the man is seen from behind and against the light, standing on dark, undulating ground. His left arm is raised in a majestic gesture as though he were directing the movements of the stars that fill the heavens, like an ideal conductor guiding his orchestra through a sidereal symphony. The colours (predominantly pinks and blues) are so beautiful, and the resultant harmony so perfect, that they seem to evoke a celestial music emanating from this peace.

Tamayo has always been a great music-lover, and he plays the guitar remarkably well. Several of his canvases represent musicians and their instruments forming a single, indivisible whole, especially in the case of that guitar which one might almost describe as part of his person. In this context it is worth recalling that it was in the company of his friend Carlos Chávez, who had become a famous composer, that Tamayo made his first journey to the United States. And it was for the National Conservatoire that he did his first mural painting when he returned. While he was working on this commission, he met a young piano student named Olga, who one year later was to become his wife — and was to share not only his life but also the beauty and intelligence of his art.

Orientation

Accompanied by Olga, Tamayo returned to New York in 1936, as one of the members of a delegation sent by the Mexican League of Revolutionary Painters and Artists. José Clemente Orozco and David Alfaro Siqueiros were also members of this delegation. Thus Tamayo participated in a collective attitude on the part of the artists of his country, despite the fact that from that moment on he adopted an absolutely personal way of seeing things and refused to submit to political dogmatism or to a realism whose laws, in his opinion, the true work of art should always be permitted to transgress.

In spite of the financial difficulties that were almost certain to beset any foreign artist in the United States during the worst years of the Depression, Tamayo and his wife decided to settle in New York City. At first he received some assistance from the organization called "Works Progress Administration" created by the U. S. Government to help young artists, but it was not long before his foreign status rendered him ineligible. Very soon, however, he was in a position to justify by his own means, and thanks to his tenacity, the risk implicit in leaving his country in search of an authentic way of expressing himself. For the unusual originality of his work quickly began to arouse interest. In 1937 he held an exhibition of gouaches, oils and drawings at Julien Levy's Gallery, and at about the same time a book on contemporary Mexican artists was published in New York, in which Tamayo figures in a prominent position. At the same time a similar book was published in Mexico by the painter Carlos Mérida, in which some comprehensive pages are devoted to Tamayo and there are reproductions of several of his works. From now on he was to have fairly regular exhibitions in various places and to see an increasing number of articles and books on him and his work. Collectors were encouraged by all this and the painter's situation became less difficult. He was also appointed teacher of art at the elegant Dalton School in New York. He was then able to rent an apartment and to acquire a studio where he continued to work indefatigably. From now on he was to live alternately in the United States and in Mexico, and New York became the place where he met all the important artists of the day, as well as the collectors, museum curators and gallery directors.

Rufino Tamayo working on the lithograph *Lobster* for Ediciones Polígrafa, Barcelona, 1973.

Tamayo's studio in his house in Mexico.

Tamayo with the French Minister for Foreign Affairs, M. Sauvanargues, at the opening of tris exhibition at the Musée d'Art Moderne de la Ville de Paris, 1974.

Tamayo receiving the medal of the *Légion d'Honneur.* On the left Dr Nabor Carrillo, Rector of the Universidad Nacional de México, and the French Ambassador.

The war years did not interrupt his work. In 1943 he painted his great mural composition in two panels for the library of Smith College, Northampton. He exhibited at the Valentine Gallery in New York every year until 1947, and after that at the Pierre Matisse. From 1946 to 1948 he also taught at the School of Fine Arts of the Brooklyn Museum. In a very few years, in fact, he had become one of the artists arousing most interest and expectation in that city which was by now, on account of the war and the influx of so many European artists, a new capital of the arts. And yet he never relinquished his constant links with his origins, and his distance from them may well have enabled him to appreciate more clearly that inexhaustible source of inspiration that he found in the Mexican climate, with its folklore, its popular traditions, its wise, reasoned, geometrical arts whose origins go back to the very beginning of time. Thanks to his profound penetration into the arcana of this past, Tamayo was already one of the very few artists, perhaps indeed the only one, to have the right to proclaim himself, in all his undertakings and in the most modern of his discoveries, essentially Mexican — and I might even go further and say essentially American. The time had come for him to embark on the adventure of conquering other continents.

Europe awaited him. Georges Wildenstein, whom he had met in New York, invited him to exhibit at his Galerie Beaux-Arts in Paris. It was just about then that this gallery, under the guidance of Raymond Cogniat, was holding authentic cycles of exhibitions that covered all the principal movements in modern painting, from Impressionism through Fauvism and Cubism down to Surrealism — and was at the same time asking the new artists who had made their reputations in other countries to come and make themselves known in Paris. The whole burden of the endeavour was borne by this private gallery, in the absence of a true museum of modern art, which was still in the fairly distant future.

One can well imagine what an event it was for Tamayo to be invited to exhibit in Paris, when he had as yet barely established a solid reputation in Mexico and New York. To mark the importance of this show, Georges Wildestein commissioned two prefaces for the catalogue:

one from Jean Cassou, who was to be the true founder of the Musée d'Art Moderne de Paris, and the other from André Breton.

I should point out that before this Paris show (which was to be prolonged by another exhibition at the Palais des Beaux-Arts in Brussels) Tamayo's works had been shown at the Venice Biennale and had been greeted there as a veritable revelation, as we can see from an important article written by Lionello Venturi, as well as favourable mentions from all the international critics. But now let us see something of what Jean Cassou wrote on the occasion of the Paris exhibition in 1950:

At the Galería Pecanins, Barcelona.

"It is not through local colour, nor yet through the expression of its contemporary epic, that we shall discover Mexico in Tamayo, but through our intuition of the deep, dark centre from which so many disturbing images come, and through the presence in these images of a spirit that is new to us: the spirit, undoubtedly, of the gods created by Tamayo's Zapotec ancestors, among which the most fascinating figure is the celebrated jade mask of the bat god of Monte Albán, the holy city. But this implies an over-precise determination and classification of the sources from which Tamayo's poetry springs, for they are scattered over a much vaster space of fables and dreams. A whole enormous prehistory, a whole mist-shrouded empire — but also a whole people, whose soul is still very much alive — have produced this art, the strangeness of which in our world confounds us. An art laden with a great mass of past and prestige, an art bearing an electric charge that makes one feel something totally different..." For Cassou the supreme virtue of Tamayo's painting is an extraordinary silence. He sees that painting "as an unknown, mysterious person who comes from far away and, under a smile as sharp as the blade of an obsidian dagger, hides what he knows and what he remembers. But what appears on the surface is shimmering and exquisite, a gossamer fabric, a phosphorescent dance. Few of the most celebrated magicians that we admire are capable of producing any enchantment to compare with the glistening nets and snares which this magical painting throws over us from its most secret depths. But as we are drawn on further, just at the edge of the abyss we see forms moving, silhouettes, evocations

Two moments of the visit paid by H. R. H. Princess Michico to the Tamayo exhibition at the Museum of Modern Art, Tokyo, 1976.

of dark gods, ideas and realities, tropical beliefs and fruit, slices of watermelon bleeding under their jade skin, gaping as wide as that archaeological grin that pursues us, like an obsession, through grisly ruins." And Cassou concludes: "Tamayo is one of the greatest poets of our time, one of the greatest poets in the world."

André Breton's preface, so important in its author's eyes that he was later to include it in the new edition of his *Surrealisme dans la peinture,* places Tamayo and his work at a universal nerve centre. According to him, Tamayo's creative processes are inspired by two vital necessities: "On the one hand, to open up once again the way of great communication of painting, as the universal language between continents that it should be, and for that purpose to prepare against the discrepancies of the vocabularies by bringing to light once more that *technical* investigation that is still the only basis for unification; on the other hand, to detach the eternal Mexico from all that may be accidental in its aspects or merely transitory in its struggles, in order to pour it into the crucible of the human soul. Thus the theme of this painting will be everyday life, noticeably more passionate than others and as though constantly goaded on by that spark of winged fire that fosters a certain distortion in the gestures and the features...; emphasized, and with its rhythm adapted, by the light. It has nothing in common with that kind of 'distortion,' always practised more or less coldly, for the empirical purposes of exaggerating the essential (Van Gogh), adapting the figures to their formats by elasticity (Matisse), replacing the finished image by its working sketch (the Cubists) or translating helplessness and anguish (Picasso, in this case making use of Expressionism). With Tamayo we find ourselves in a trembling world, in which man has remained directly linked to the forces of nature and the morphology is conditioned more than anywhere else by ecology."

Finally, Raymond Cogniat wrote the first work in French devoted to Tamayo and his oeuvre (Presses Litteraires de France, 1951). Cogniat sees Tamayo as a sort of demigod calmly dominating a demoniac universe, with a poetry made of passion and restraint, of violence and reason. Cogniat expresses his admiration for Tamayo's work, his comprehension, even his suport, while at the same time underlining the fundamental difference between it and other great works of today: "We cannot claim this work as belonging to our world; its construction cannot be compared with that of Cubism, for it lacks the latter's serenity; the intensity of Tamayo's palette has nothing to do with the fauvist theories about pure colour and the complementary accords; abstract art loses its rights in the face of this painter's urge to create not signs but living creatures; his violence has no point of contact with that of the Expressionists and his exasperation is not of the same order. And however instinctive he may be, there is nothing in his work that might let him pass for a naïve painter, while nature herself in that work loses her rights to realism."

This "difference" of Tamayo can be explained by the knowledge he has acquired of the values of western art. He himself admitted to his friend and compatriot Octavio Paz, who has written an excellent book and several articles and essays on his work, that he had learned a great deal from the moderating influence of Braque, who had taught him restraint and rigorousness. "The presence of Braque," writes Paz, "did not take the form of an imitation or a contagion, but of a lesson." One does not find it so much in Tamayo's actual paintings as in his general attitude to painting regarded as a universe of solely plastic correspondences.

Venturi had already rightly observed that if Tamayo has remained so closely bound to his native land and its ancient cultures, even more so than any other Mexican, it is because he has been able to develop and broaden his repertoire and his style thanks to his assimilation of the experiments of Gauguin and Picasso, and also thanks to the experiments he himself carried out in the United States. "His refinement expresses a poetic distancing that makes his images a sort of fable." In fact there was a secret kinship between the very foundations of pre-Columbian sculpture — with the strict geometry of its conceptions, the solidity of its volumes and its extraordinary fidelity to its material — and the requirements imposed by the perceptive visionaries of Cubism and Abstract Art. Tamayo's art, which drinks from the sources of the past

Tamayo at the reception held in his honour at the
45th São Paulo Biennale, 1977.

and assimilates the lessons of the present, succeeds in achieving an extraordinary synthesis, at once logical and poetic, of forms, lines and volumes. As Octavio Paz has written, "the symbolism of ancient art is transformed into *transfiguration* in the painting of Tamayo. The Meso-American tradition has shown him, even more vigorously than Klee and the Surrealists, that the plastic object is a high-frequencey station transmitting multiple meanings and images."

One might say that, in the same way as pre-Columbian art, Tamayo's painting is at the same time metaphor, geometry and transfiguration. So much, at least, is true of its constitution, its structure. This painting, however, is endowed with a covering that is absolutely exclusive to it: its bones show through, or are intuitively perceived, under a magical living skin which belongs to it alone and which is expressed by the painter's extraordinary invention of colour.

Mutations and chemistry

In the beginnings of Tamayo's development of a personal style of painting, he concentrated principally on the human figures which surrounded him: the outlines of his family or the local people, or the colourful, juicy images of the fruit of his country. Even at that early age he knew how to make good use of the contrast between the wealth of light-filled colour, and the white cloths that he saw in the kitchen or the market stalls, and the sobriety and simplicity of dark everyday clothing. Looking at these images which, though still static, are nevertheless loaded with an internal weight and with the possibility of mutations, it is quite evident that nothing in them corresponds to the investigations then being carried out by painters in an effort to represent movement and external events, or to evoke historic figures, even from contemporary history.

Tamayo receiving an honorary doctorate at the Universidad Nacional Autónoma de México, 1979.

This early work, however, was quite soon to be invaded by disturbing elements in the form of animals in motion — their feet thrust forward, their toothless mouths opened wide — seen from sharp-angled perspectives and with distortions that usually anticipate an analogous treatment to which his human figures were to be subjected. As examples I might mention the 1941 canvas entitled *Animals* in the New York Museum of Modern Art (Two horrible, half-starved dogs, howling to the heavens), or his *Coyote* in the Metropolitan Museum of Art, also in New York. Pre-Columbian sculpture abounds in animals of this sort and evidently provided one of the sources of Tamayo's inspiration. But when he spoke of these beasts in a conversation with Emily Genauer, Tamayo said that he had also been thinking of the forms used in folk art, which are certainly rather similar. And in the feeling of anguish that he had expressed through those animals howling in despair, might there not also have been an echo of the dramatic situation the world was suffering at that time?

At a reception held in his honour in the Domecq Cellars, 1979.

Very soon afterwards Tamayo was to project these themes into space, where an ascendant impulse seems to raise them to the stars of the day and the night, which lure them with cries and gestures. And thus, very quickly, we are granted a prefiguration of the metamorphoses that were to be revealed by future moments in the artist's creative life:

In his house in Mexico in 1979.

characters drawn up by a sort of cosmic vibration, presenting their different aspects as they stretch out before us, opening their hearts and their entrails. In fact it is Tamayo's creation itself that is suffering its war and its cataclysm. Man here is a shattered, dismembered figure that is confronted with the mysteries of the cosmos and has become the prey of invisible and uncontrollable forces. If hitherto he was the centre of the universe, now we suddenly see him dislodged, displaced, dislocated, carried off by a whirlwind of elements. Now indeed vulnerable, he is exposed to all aggressions. Despair and madness are all that lie in wait for him.

A work in the Cleveland Museum, entitled *Women Reaching for the Moon* (1946), shows us figures leaping free from an earth giving way beneath them and performing an insensate action in their desire of the absolute. The space here is not yet a total void: there are some constellations shining still over geometrical forms that resemble glass rocks. In such a world the characters cry out in despair (as in *The Shout,* 1947, in the Galleria Nazionale d'Art Moderna in Rome) or suffer atrocious tortures *(The Tormented,* 1949, Private collection, Japan); they become monsters with sharp, cutting shapes and imploring eyes. The subject is repeated in the 1954 *Cosmic Terror* (Museo Nacional de Arte, Mexico City): a man hurls his cry forth into the vast silence of space. Forms evoking sharp, cutting scythes appear in a series of canvases like *Man Opening His Heart* (1954), *The Burning Man* (1955) or *The Astronomer* (1954, Emily Genauer Collection, New York), in which, in the middle of a swirling spiral that is meant to evoke heaven knows what exploration of space, we see a red circle that resembles a beating heart. These are mysterious works, and undoubtedly premonitory, in which the artist expresses the fear that man may finally be the victim of his own incessant conquests.

The figures, at first sombre, gradually grow brighter. There may at times be nothing left but the structure, just as it is sufficient for a limb to be represented by its stump. The shadow of the bone is perceived through the flesh. The whole world around us is dislocated in similar fashion, and its fragments are revealed in the infinitesimal splinters piercing the cloudy atmosphere. The little beings peopling the universe spring up, their arms stretching out before them, their rounded heads split open like fruit. One might be tempted to think that in these works the being is no longer personified, that everything blends indistinctly into the landscape. But nothing could be further from the truth. In these works, in fact, not one of the elements that go to make them up has been forgotten. The characteristic features reappear, and are all the more striking for being restored within a disturbed order.

Tamayo and Olga, 1979.

Tamayo was likewise to become an astonishing portrait artist. At several stages in his career, for instance, he has painted admirable portraits of his wife, Olga. Also worthy of consideration in this context is the extraordinary documentation he produced of his encounter with Jean Dubuffet. In the portrait he painted of that artist, every detail is heightened and defined independently, with the result that the whole acquires a character that goes beyond any normal human structure.

a

b

c

d

Fulfilment

Once it has been taken back to its embryonic forms, every creature, whether man or animal, is capable of developing afresh from itself and the qualities that define it. And it will then develop spontaneously and unexpectedly, as though it were the result not only of a synthesis or a previous decision but also of a natural, spontaneous evolution. This will only have been possible because the embryo to which the creature has been returned has finally found once more a beneficent climate in which all its possibilities of existing have again taken shape. In the case which now concerns us, this substance is evidently Tamayo's extraordinary colour, that colour which is the very blood of his creation.

Beginning with his earliest works in New York, Tamayo's art soon asserted itself and his palette already foreshadowed that wealth of colour that from then on was to characterize all his work, eventually leading to the sovereign clearness and luminosity that would be

f

predominant as from 1950. But even an examination of any of those early pictures can teach us a lot. Thus, for instance, the 1929 still life entitled *Yellow Chair,* despite the smallness of its dimensions, is so very perfectly organized that it gives an absolutely monumental impression. The superbly coloured masses of the fruit and the fabric on which it lies, together with the fruit bowl resting against the chair itself, form a triangular composition in which the rigorously delimited planes have been modelled with an enormously sensuous feeling. And this pyramid, with its delicately articulated planes, is severely framed by the uprights and crossbars of the chair, the yellow stain of which is carefully set against the dark red background of the picture.

Another painting that might be mentioned along with this one, as being very close to it in feeling, is *Mandolines and Pineapples,* painted in 1930 and immediately purchased for the Phillips Collection in Washington.

a and b. With the President of Mexico, Lic. José López Portillo, at the opening of the Museo Rufino Tamayo, Mexico City.

c. Tamayo during the speech made handing over his Museum to the Mexican people.

d. Entrance to the Museo Rufino Tamayo.

e. Painting room.

f. Sculpture room.

Tamayo handing over the key of his museum (the Museo de Arte Prehistórico Rufino Tamayo) to Lic. Fernando Gómez Sandoval, Governor of Oaxaca, Mexico.

One of the rooms in the Museo de Arte Prehistórico Rufino Tamayo, Oaxaca, Mexico.

The elements in this composition that give it its title, seen between the blue leaves of a double door, are as it were the culminating point in the investigations of Tamayo's early period. The colour becomes increasingly more subtle until, without in the least diminishing their strength, it gives fine nuances to the most surprising contrasts. The familiar fruit, solid and heavy, permits all the sweetness of its flesh to show thorugh. The luminous rind glistens with a thousand flashes, the heat of which is tempered by the cold proximity of the blues and greens. One might almost say that the palpitating life of these pineapples gives a particularly sonorous quality to the musical instruments accompanying them. The opulence of the hot country is exalted in the penumbra.

So great is the unity of thought in Tamayo, so constant the firmness of his drawing, that one can pass on directly to his most recent works, even though we shall be skipping the best part of his investigations:

his experiences with murals and all those things of which he has made such abundant use. It seems as though he has only very slowly acquired greater subtlety and refinement in his colours, particularly in his use of red, that colour which is so often predominant that the artist mentions it in his titles, but which might really be better described as a sort of implicit permanence underlying everything that comes from his brush. Whether it be the *Couple in Red,* painted in 1961, the 1963 *Man with Red Hat,* with its crimsons, scarlets, purples and mauves so well distributed by the sombre drawing, or the *Three Figures in Red* (1963), with its characters drawn in parallel lines that recall the ringed bodies of wasps, it is quite clear to be seen that red is the ingredient that nourishes the atmosphere in which the artist's creation moves. And what can we say of all the fruit — all the watermelons that he has painted, from the juiciest and most substantial to those so spectral that they are almost abstract — except that they, too, are symbols of that purest joy that gives life to Tamayo's work and guides it?

That being the case, the representation of the characters can be reduced to the most elementary of themes, to the circle or the square. It is sufficient for the junction with the body to be marked by a sign in the form of a T, representing at once the eyes and the neck. The figures thus become spectral, as though seen on a fluoroscope. Over the years such pictures as *Portrait of a Child* (1964), *Man's Torso* (1970) and *Man in Red and Green* (1975) mark the permanence of this evolution, so closely linked to time and so far removed from any earthly attachment. And canvases like *Two Figures and the Moon* (1970), in which all the shades of pink and blue give some body to the geometrical characters, are like the culminating point of a harmony and refinement that are reminiscent of some of the works of Klee.

The theme of the figure treated in the form of an articulated doll, with its torso slashed by transversal bars, was frequently repeated, as may be seen in *Children in Red* (1973), *The Great Galaxy* (1978) and *Standing Woman* (1978). From his early colours, so bright and strongly contrasted, he has arrived at a more muted, less crowded palette, but one which is as rich and fertile as ever. For this has always been his great art: with only a few colours, but making use of the full range of each and endowing them all with an infinite variety of shades, he creates that effect of richness and completeness that impresses us so greatly. Even in those works in which the variations of green and blue are multiplied, his incomparable red ochre never fails to appear and triumph over the rest.

But if the sun is his source, he has still had to discover or possess the material that is capable of capturing that heat and that light and of giving them body. I am convinced that Tamayo has rediscovered, probably without even realizing it — perhaps it was the privilege of his heredity — the equivalent of that substance which our prehistoric ancestors, whether in America, Europe or Africa, smeared on the walls of the caves that gave them shelter. I came to this conclusion quite recently when I witnessed the appearance, in a film about the Olmec grottoes, of some little mural paintings which immediately reminded me of figures from the caves of Périgord with which I was already familiar. *Apparitions* is the exact word that I would use to define those figures emerging from a sort of dust haze (probably caused by the application of identical pigments); and it is also the most suitable word to translate the impression I felt, over thirty years ago now, when I first saw the paintings of Tamayo and tried in vain to discover what it was that they reminded me of.

One may attempt to define the creative process in Tamayo, a process that has no equal among the artists of today, as a return to the primordial forms, the definition of embryos which, on being placed in a nutritive liquid, will find their complete natural development. The idea is prolonged in itself; its essence is propagated. Can there be a greater fulfilment? Art is concerned with a deeper truth than appearance, a truth that is previous to the forms it has already taken. The truth is the result of its own prerequisite. Art expresses the primordial.

Jacques Lassaigne (1982)

1
Boy in Blue (Niño en azul). 1928.
Oil on canvas, 29½ × 25⅛ in. (75 × 63.8 cm).
Olga Tamayo Collection, Mexico City.

2

4

3

2
Arrangement of objects (Arreglo de objetos). 1928.
Oil on canvas, 19¾×25⅝ in. (50×65 cm).
Bernard Lewin Collection, Los Angeles, California.

3
Still life (Naturaleza muerta). 1928.
Oil on canvas, 22½×18¾ in. (57×47.5 cm).
Bernard Lewin Collection, Los Angeles, California.

4
Shells (Los caracoles). 1929.
Oil on canvas, 23¾×24¾ in. (59×63 cm).
Olga Tamayo Collection, Mexico City.

5
Yellow Chair (Silla amarilla). 1929.
Oil on canvas, 28¾×25 in. (73×63.5 cm).
Olga Tamayo Collection, Mexico City.

6

6
Mandolines and Pineapples (Mandolinas y piñas).
1930.
Oil on canvas, 19¾ 3 27⅝ in. (50.2 3 70 cm).
The Phillips Collection, Washington, D.C.

7
Nude in Grey (Desnudo en gris). 1931.
Oil on canvas, 35 3 25¼ in. (89 3 64 cm).
Museo de Arte Moderno/I.N.B.A., Mexico City.

7

8

8
Homage to Juárez (Homenaje a Juárez). 1932.
Oil on canvas, 23⅝ × 29½ in. (60 × 75 cm).
Museo de Arte Moderno/I.N.B.A., Mexico City.

9
Homage to Zapata (Homenaje a Zapata). 1935.
Oil on canvas, 25⅝ × 21¾ in. (65 × 54 cm).
Mr and Mrs Herman Weitz Collection, Mexico City.

9

10

11

12

10
Photogenic Venus (Venus fotogénica). 1934.
Oil on canvas, 29¹/₂×39³/₈ in. (75×100 cm).
Secretaría de Hacienda y Crédito Público, Mexico City.

11
The Musicians (Los músicos). 1934.
Oil on canvas, 31¹/₂×39³/₈ in. (80×100 cm).
Cummins Catherwood Collection, Saratoga Springs, N.Y.

12
Still Life (Naturaleza muerta). 1937.
Oil on canvas, 39³/₈×53¹/₈ in. (100×135 cm).
Robert Brady Foundation, Cuernavaca, Mexico.

13

13
Fruit Vendors (Vendedoras de fruta). 1938.
Oil on canvas, 17¼×23¾ in. (43.8×60.3 cm).
Zuinaga Aguilar de García Collection Mexico City.

14
Women of Tehuantepec (Mujeres de Tehuantepec).
1939.
Oil on canvas, 34¼×57⅛ in. (87×145 cm).
Albright-Knox Art Gallery, Buffalo, N.Y.

15

16

18

19

18
Two Dogs (Dos perros). 1941.
Oil on canvas, 31½×40¼ in. (76.9×102.3 cm).
Museum of Modern Art, Houston, Texas.

19
Lion and Horse (León y caballo). 1942.
Oil on canvas, 36×46 in. (91.5×116.8 cm).
Washington University Gallery of Art,
St. Louis Missouri.

20
Animals (Animales). 1941.
Oil on canvas, 30³⁄₈ × 39³⁄₈ in. (77 × 100 cm).
The Museum of Modern Art, New York.

21
Woman Calling (Mujer llamando). 1941.
Oil on canvas, 36×24 in. (91.5×61 cm).
Lee A. Ault Collection, New York.

21

22

22
*Two Galloping Horses in Red and Brown
(Dos caballos corriendo, en rojo y café)*. 1942.
Oil on canvas, 34 × 46¾ in. (86.2 × 118.8 cm).
Private collection, Monterrey.

23
Woman Spinning (Mujer hilando). 1943.
Oil on canvas, 42 × 33 in. (106.7 × 83.9 cm).
Roy R. Newberger Collection.

23

24
*Nature and the Artist - The Work of Art and the
Observer (La naturaleza y el artista - La obra de arte
y el espectador).* 1943.
Fresco, at present transferred by means of strappo
technic to 22 moving panels,
9 ft. 8½ in. × 43 ft., 6⅞ in. (2.95 × 13.28 m).
Hillyer Library, Smith College Massachusetts.
Commissioned to the artist by Jere Abbot in honour
of Mrs Elizabeth Cutter Morrow.

25
The Flute-Player (El flautista). 1944.
Oil on canvas, 45 × 37¼ in. (114.4 × 94.5 cm).
IBM Corporation, Armonk, N.Y.

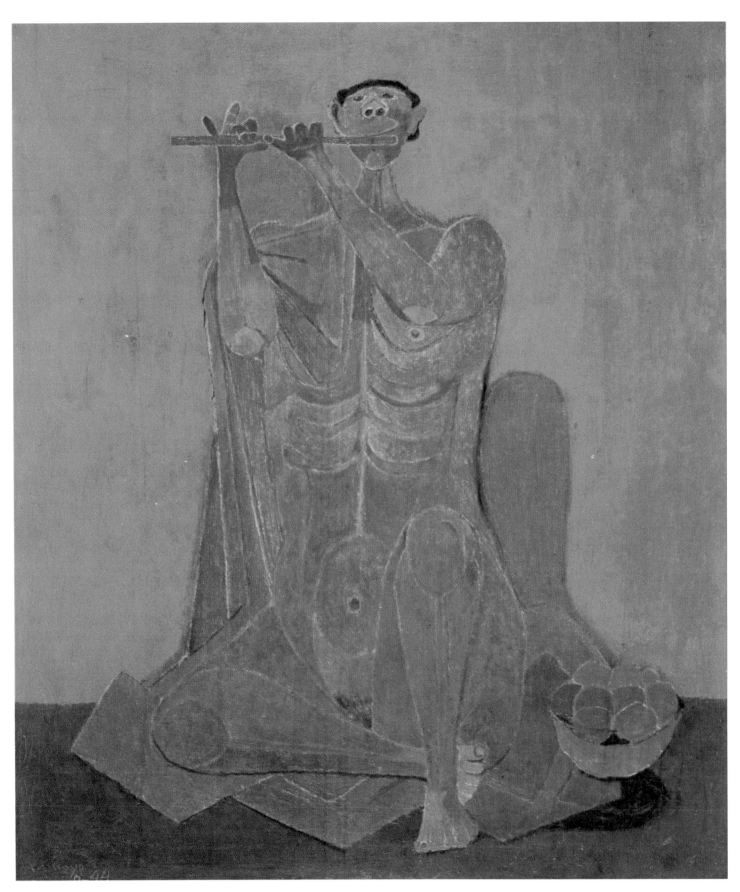

Bird Charmer (Encantador de pájaros). 1945.
Oil on canvas, 61 × 50¾ in. (155 × 129 cm).
Private collection, New York.

27

28

27
Woman Dressing Her Hair (Mujer arreglándose el pelo). 1944.
Gouache, 29 × 22⅞ in. (73.5 × 58 cm).
Private collection, U.S.A.

28
Woman and Bird (Mujer y pájaro). 1944.
Oil on canvas, 42 × 34 in. (106.7 × 86.3 cm).
The Cleveland Museum of Art. Leonard C. Hanna Jr. Collection, Cleveland, Ohio.

29
Portrait of Olga (Retrato de Olga). 1945.
Oil on canvas, 48 × 35 in. (122 × 89 cm).
Mr and Mrs Ralph F. Colin Collection, New York.

29

30

31

30
Women Reaching for the Moon (Mujeres alcanzando la luna). 1946.
Oil on canvas, 36¼×26 in. (92×66 cm).
The Cleveland Museum of Art. Donated by the Leonard C. Hanna Fund, Cleveland, Ohio.

31
Dancers Over the Sea (Danzantes frente al mar).
1945.
Oil on canvas, 30×40 in. (76.2×101.6 cm).
Cincinnati Art Museum. Donated by Mr Lee Ault,
Cincinnati, Ohio.

32
Total Eclipse (Eclipse total). 1946.
Oil on canvas, 40 × 30 in.
(101.6 × 76.2 cm).
Fogg Art Museum, Harvard Universi
Cambridge, Massachusetts.

3

The Shout (El grito). 1947.
Oil on canvas, 40 × 30 in.
(101.6 × 76.2 cm).
Galleria Nazionale d'Arte Moderna,
Rome.

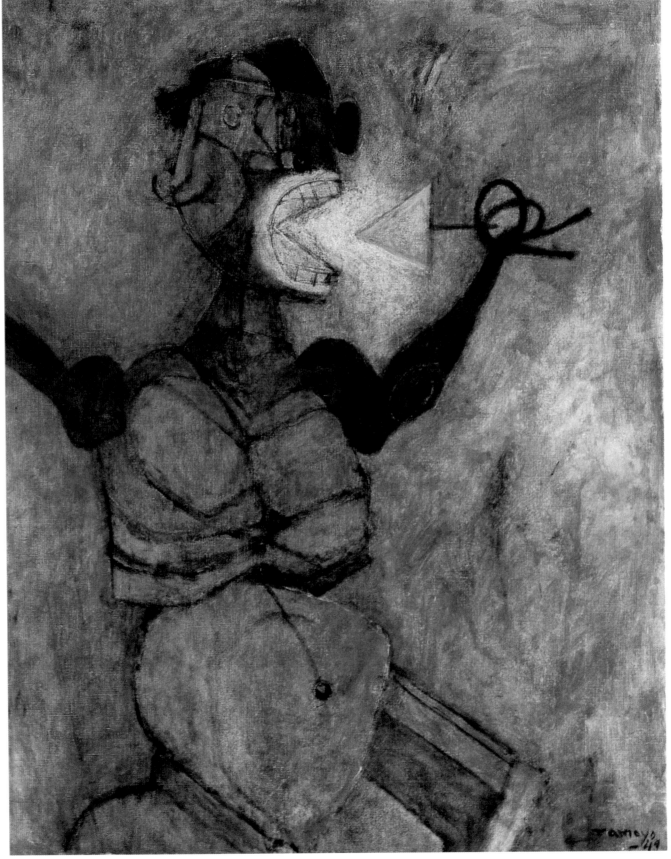

35

34
Lollipop (Piruli). 1949.
Oil on canvas, 38⅝ × 31½ in. (98 × 80 cm).
Mr and Mrs Stephen Simon Collection, New York.

35
Man Before the Infinite (El hombre ante el infinito).
1950.
Oil on canvas, 37⅜ × 53⅛ in. (95 × 135 cm).
Musées Royaux des Beaux-Arts, Brussels.

37

38

36
Man with Guitar (Hombre con guitarra). 1950.
Oil on canvas, 76¾ × 51¼ in. (195 × 130 cm).
Musée National d'Art Moderne, Centre d'Art et de
Culture Georges Pompidou, Paris.

37
The Tormented (El atormentado). 1949
Oil on canvas, 39⅜ × 31½ in. (100 × 80 cm).
Private collection, Japan.

38
Man with Cigar (Hombre con puro). 1950.
Oil on canvas, 32⅛ × 25¾ in. (81.5 × 65.5 cm).
Mr and Mrs Stephen Simon Collection, New York.

39

39
Nude in White (Desnudo en blanco). 1950.
Oil on canvas, 76⅜×50¾ in. (194×129 cm).
Mr and Mrs Harry Pollack Collection, Longboat Key,
Florida.

40
Cow Swatting Flies (Vaca espantándose las moscas).
1951.
Oil on canvas, 31⅛×39 in. (79×99 cm).
Humanities Research Center, The University of Texas,
Austin, Texas.

40

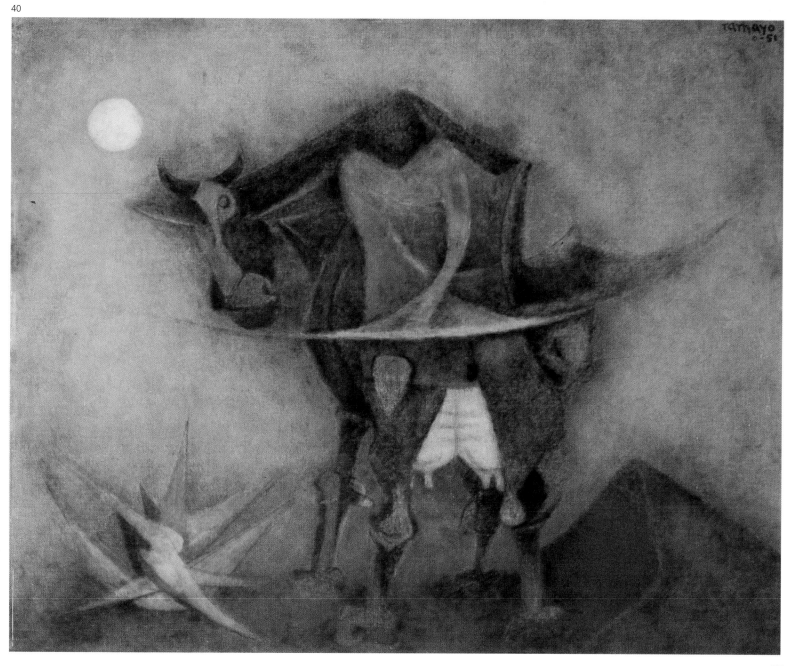

41
Homage to the Indian Race (Homenaje a la raza india). 1952.
Vinelita on celotex, 196⅞ × 157½ in. (500 × 400 cm)
Museo Rufino Tamayo/I.N.B.A., Mexico City.

42

42
Sunset (Anochecer). 1953.
Oil on masonite, 11¾×31½ in. (29.8×80 cm).
Private Collection.

43
Supersonic Plane (Avión más rápido que el sonido).
1954.
Oil on canvas, 21¼×29½ in. (54×75 cm).
Dr Jaime Constantiner Collection, Mexico.

43

44

45

44
The Burning Man (El quemado). 1955.
Oil on canvas, 39³⁄₈×31½ in. (100×80 cm).
Rogerio and Lorenza Azcárraga Collection,
Mexico City.

45
Cosmic Terror (Terror cósmico). 1954.
Oil on canvas, 41³⁄₄×30 in. (106×76 cm).
Museo de Arte Moderno/I.N.B.A., Mexico City.

46
Telephonitis (Telefonitis). 1957.
Oil in canvas, 39³⁄₈×32 in. (100×81.3 cm).
Nasjonalgalleriet, Oslo.

47

47
White Watermelons (Sandías en blanco). 1956.
Oil on canvas, 31½ × 39⅜ in. (80 × 100 cm).
Olga Azcárraga Collection, Mexico City.

48
Night of Mysteries (Noche de misterios). 1957.
Oil on canvas, 39⅜ × 32 in. (100 × 81.3 cm).
Nasjonalgalleriet, Oslo.

48

49

49
Insomnia (Insomnio). 1958.
Oil on canvas, 38½ × 57⅛ in. (97.8 × 145 cm).
Francisco Osio Morales Collection, Mexico City.

50
Prometheus Bringing Fire to Mankind (Prometeo entregando el fuego a los hombres). 1958.
Fresco 196⅞ × 177 in. (500 × 450 cm).
Lecture Hall, UNESCO, Paris.

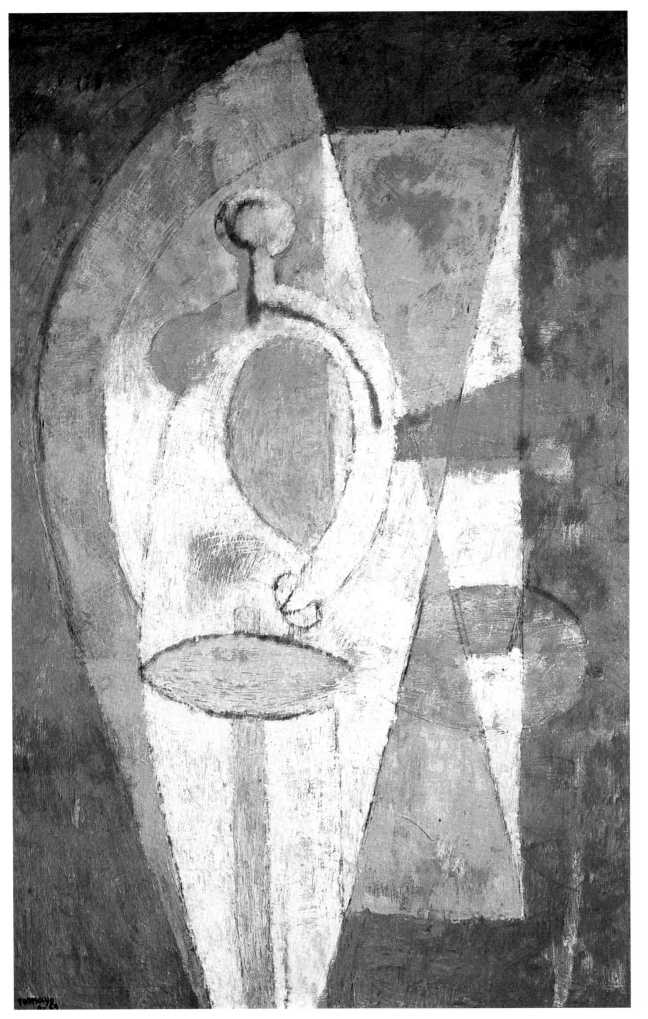

51
Woman in White (Mujer en blanco).
Oil on canvas, 76¾ × 51¼ in.
(195 × 130 cm).
Milwaukee Art Center.
Donated by Mr and Mrs Harry L. Bra
Milwaukee, Wisconsin.

man in Grey (Mujer en gris). 1959.
on canvas, 76¾ × 51¼ in.
⊃ × 130 cm).
Solomon R. Guggenheim Museum,
York.

53

53
Children Playing (Niños jugando). 1959.
Oil on canvas, 51¼×76¾ in. (130.2×195 cm).
Mr and Mrs Ralph F. Collin Collection, New York.

54
Man with a Guitar (Hombre con una guitarra).
1959.
Oil on canvas, 37⅜×53⅛ in. (95×135 cm).
Private collection, U.S.A.

55

55
Children's Game (Juego de niños). 1960.
Oil on canvas, 53⅛ × 76¾ in. (135 × 195 cm).
Rafaela Arocena de Ussía Collection, Paris.

56
Man with Flower (Hombre con flor). 1960.
Oil on canvas, 50½ × 38 in. (128.3 × 96.5 cm).
Hannelore B. Chulhof Collection, New York.

57

57
Composition (Composición). 1960.
Oil on canvas, 37³⁄₈×53¹⁄₈ in. (95×135 cm).
Musée National d'Art Moderne, Centre d'Art et de
Culture Georges Pompidou, Paris.

58
The Coffeepot (La cafetera). 1960.
Oil on canvas, 53¹⁄₈×76³⁄₄ in. (135×195 cm).
Bernard Lewin Collection, Los Angeles, California.

58

59
Women (Mujeres). 1960.
Oil on canvas, 54 × 76¾ in. (137 × 195 cm).
Arnold and Elaine Horwitch Collection, Phoenix,
Arizona.

60
Two Characters (Dos personajes). 1961.
Oil on canvas, 37⅜ × 51¼ in. (95 × 130 cm).
Mimi Indaco Collection, Mexico.

59

61

62

64

63
Two Figures in Blue (Dos figuras en azul). 1961.
Oil on canvas, 31⅞ × 39⅜ in. (81 × 100 cm).
Museo de Bellas Artes, Caracas.

64
Couple in Red (Pareja en rojo). 1961.
Oil on canvas, 38⅝ × 51⅝ in. (98 × 131 cm).
Jorge Díaz Serrano Collection, Mexico City.

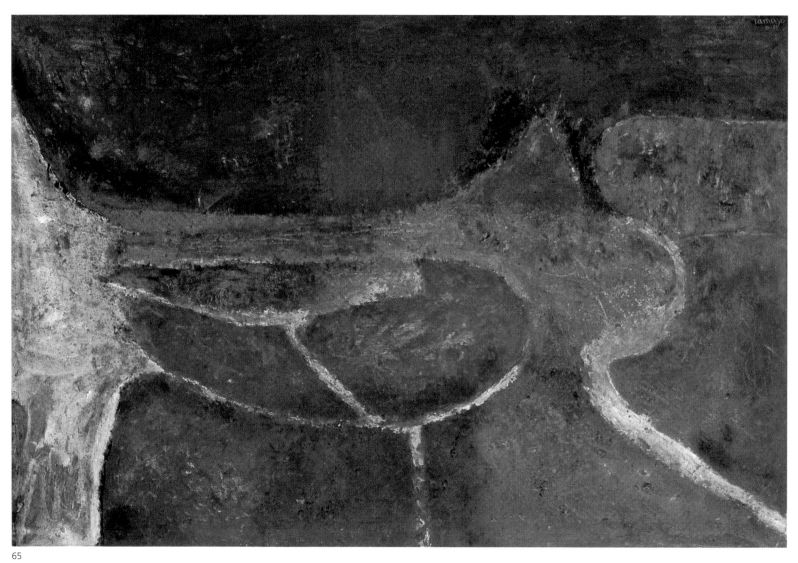

65

65
Mountainous Landscape (Paisaje serrano). 1961.
Oil on canvas, 53⅛×76¾ in. (135×195 cm).
Museo de Arte Moderno/I.N.B.A., Mexico City.

66
Meeting (Encuentro). 1961.
Oil on canvas, 53⅛×76¾ in. (135×195 cm).
Museo de Arte Moderno/I.N.B.A., Mexico City.

66

67
Figure (Figura). 1961.
Oil on canvas, 17³/₄×21⁵/₈ in. (45×55 cm).
Bernard Lewin Collection, Los Angeles, California

68
Head with Blue Hat (Cabeza con sombrero azul).
1962.
Oil on canvas, 15³/₄×19³/₄ in. (40×50 cm).
Bernard Lewin Collection, Los Angeles, California

69
Woman in Front of a Looking-Glass (Mujer ante el espejo). 1961.
Oil on canvas, 39³/₈×31¹/₂ in. (100×80 cm).
Private collection, Mexico City.

70

70
Winding Road (Camino sinuoso). 1962.
Oil on canvas, 31⅞ × 39⅜ in. (81 × 100 cm).
Pivate collection, Mexico City.

71
Afternoon Sun (Sol de tarde). 1962.
Oil on canvas, 31½ × 39⅜ in. (80 × 100 cm).
Neda Anhalt Collection, Mexico City.

71

72

72
Man's Profile (Perfil de hombre). 1962.
Oil on canvas, 31½ × 39⅜ in. (80 × 100 cm).
Private collection, Mexico.

73
Two figures (Dos figuras). 1962.
Oil on canvas, 39⅜ × 29½ in. (100 × 75 cm).
Private collection, Mexico City.

74
*Three Characters and a Bird (Tres personajes
y un pájaro)*. 1962.
Oil on canvas, 53⅛×76¾ in. (135×195 cm).
Museo de Arte Moderno/I.N.B.A., Mexico City.

75
Taurus (Tauro). 1962.
Oil on canvas, 38¼×51¼ in. (97×130 cm).
Bernard Lewin Collection, Los Angeles, California.

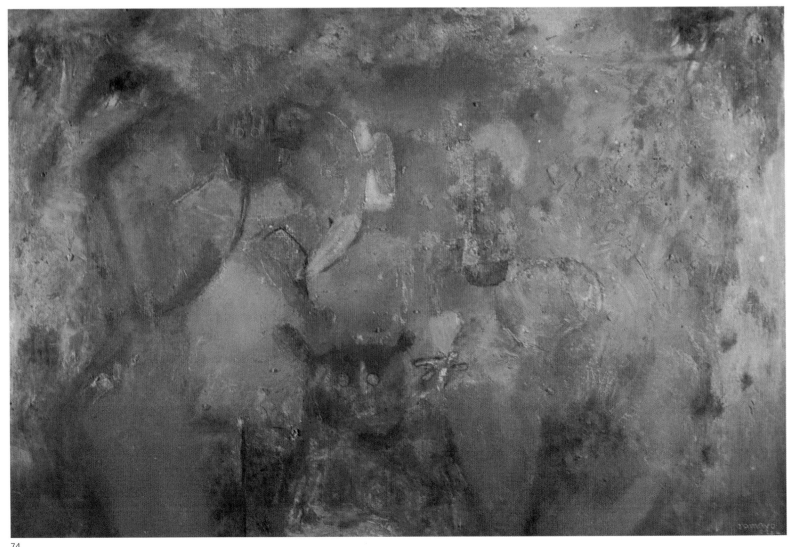

74

77

76
Man with Red Hat (Hombre con sombrero rojo).
1963.
Oil on canvas, 51⅝×38¼ in. (131×97.2 cm).
Museo de Arte Moderno/I.N.B.A., Mexico City.

77
Two Characters (Dos personajes). 1967.
Oil on canvas, 39⅜×31½ in. (100×80 cm).
Dorsky Gallery, New York.

78

79

78
Boy at the Window (Muchacho en la ventana).
1963.
Oil on canvas, 18⅞×25⅝ in. (48×65 cm).
Bernard Lewin Collection, Los Angeles, California.

79
Man (Hombre). 1961.
Oil on canvas, 29½×36⅝ in. (75×93 cm).
Knoedler Gallery, New York.

80
Black Venus (Venus negra). 1965.
Oil on canvas, 39⅜×32 in. (100×81.2 cm).
Private collection, Mexico City.

81
Couple (Pareja). 1965.
Oil on canvas, 39⅜ × 31½ in. (100 × 80 cm).
Eli Klein Collection, Mexico.

82
The Smoker (El fumador). 1965.
Oil on canvas, 31½ × 26⅜ in. (80 × 67 cm).
Angel Céspedes Collection, Mexico.

83
Portrait of Olga (Retrato de Olga). 1964.
Oil on canvas, 82⅝ × 53⅛ in. (210 × 135 cm).
Museo Rufino Tamayo/l.N.B.A., Mexico City.

81

82

83

84

84
Family (Familia). 1965.
Oil on canvas, 31½×39⅜ in. (80×100 cm).
Licio Lagos Collection, Mexico.

85
Portrait of Boys (Retrato de muchachos). 1966.
Oil on canvas, 37⅞×53⅛ in. (95×135 cm).
Mayalen Zunzunegui Collection, Mexico.

86
The Juggler (El juglar). 1966.
Oil on canvas, 31½×39⅜ in. (80×100 cm).
Ana Misrachi Collection, Mexico.

85

86

129

87

87
Couple in the Garden (Pareja en el jardín). 1966.
Oil on canvas, 53⅛ × 76¾ in. (135 × 195 cm).
Fernando Casas Bernard Collection, Mexico City.

88
Dancers (Danzantes). 1966.
Oil on canvas, 51¼ × 76¾ in. (130 × 195 cm).
Mr and Mrs Leon Davidoff Collection, Mexico City.

88

89

89
Three Women (Tres mujeres). 1966.
Oil on canvas, 38¼×51¼ in. (97×130 cm).
Jaime Constantiner Collection, Mexico.

90
The Man with the Stick (Hombre del bastón). 1966.
Oil on canvas, 38¾×31½ in. (98.5×80 cm).
René Becerra Collection, Mexico City.

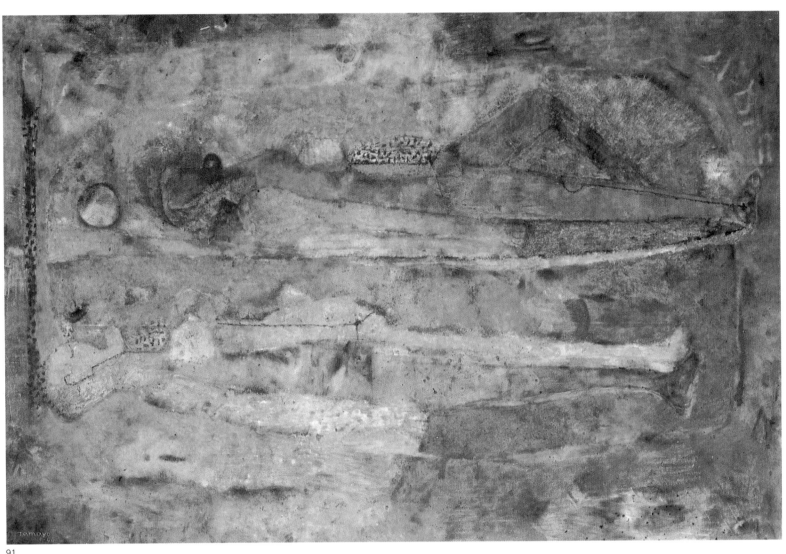

91

91
Women in Repose (Mujeres en reposo). 1966.
Oil on canvas, 53⅛ × 76¾ in. (135 × 195 cm).
Carlos Hank Rohn Collection, Mexico.

92
Self-Portrait (Autorretrato). 1967.
Oil on canvas, 68⅞ × 49¼ in. (175 × 125 cm).
Museo de Arte Moderno/I.N.B.A., Mexico City.

93

93
Three Women in Profile (Tres mujeres de perfil).
1967.
Oil on canvas, 51¼ × 76¾ in. (130 × 195 cm).
Lina Klein Collection, Mexico.

94
Carnival (Carnaval). 1967.
Oil on canvas 53⅛ × 37⅜ in.(135 × 95 cm).
Private collection, Monterrey.

94

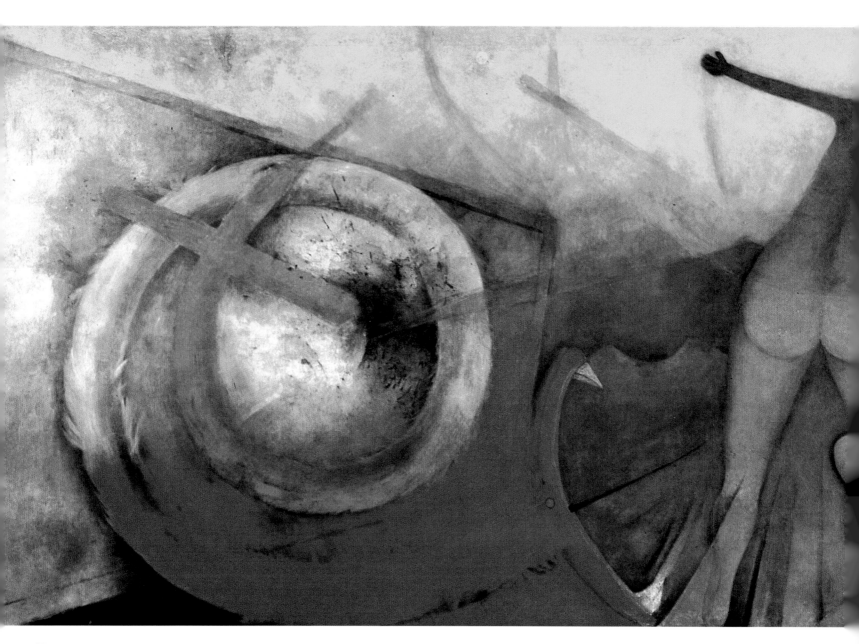

95
*The Mexican and His World (El mexicano
y su mundo)*. 1967.
Mural, 196⅞×53⅛ in. (500×135 cm).
Secretaría de Relaciones Exteriores, Mexico City.

96
*The Mexican and His World (El mexicano
y su mundo)* (detall). 1967.
Mural, 196⅞ × 53⅛ in. (500 × 135 cm).
Secretaría de Relaciones Exteriores, Mexico City

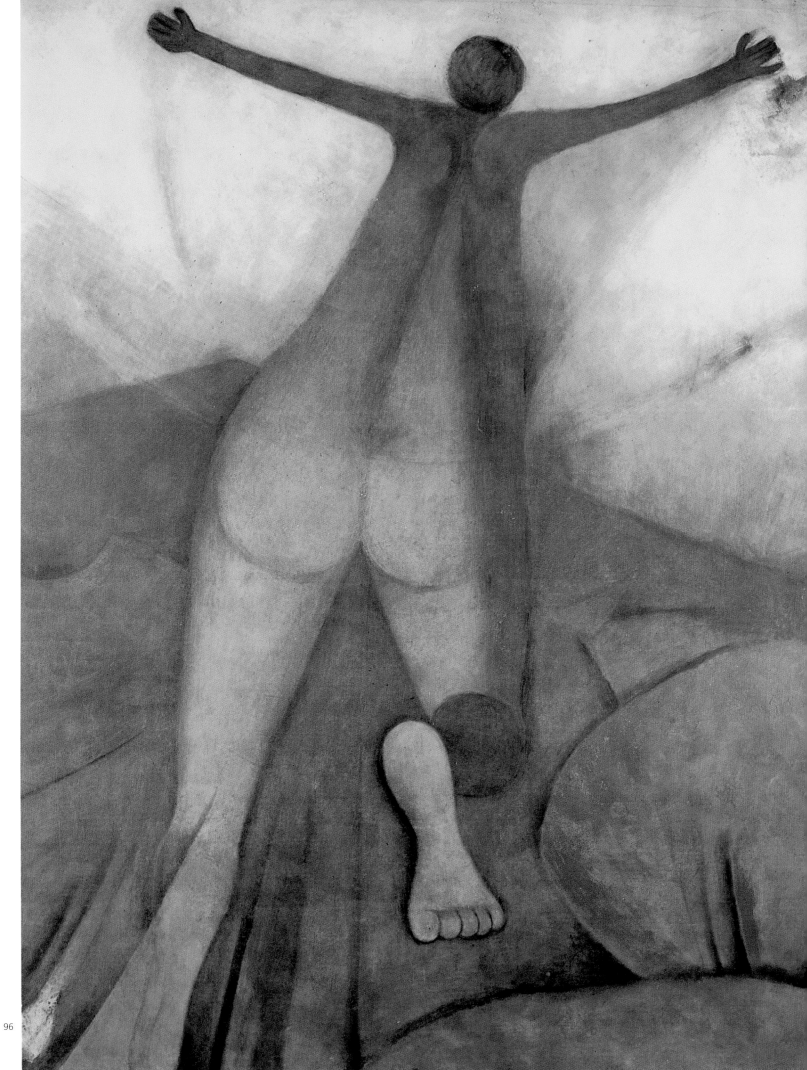

97
Three Figures (Tres figuras). 1966.
Oil on canvas, 51¼ × 76¾ in. (130 × 195 cm).
Moisés Tanur Collection, Mexico City.

98
Three Figures in Red (Tres figuras en rojo). 1967.
Oil on canvas, 53⅛ × 76¾ in. (135 × 195 cm).
José Guindi Collection, Mexico.

97

99

99
Man with Big Hat (Hombre con gran sombrero).
1967.
Oil on canvas, 31½ × 39⅜ in. (80 × 100 cm).
Private Collection, Miami, Florida.

100
Marriage Portrait (Retrato matrimonial). 1967.
Oil on canvas, 53½ × 76¾ in. (136 × 195 cm).
Bernard Lewin Collection, Los Angeles, California.

100

101
Total Eclipse (Eclipse total). 1967.
Oil on canvas, 13 × 21⅝ in. (33 × 55 cm).
Rodney Madeiros Collection, San Francisco.

102
Three Characters in Red (Tres personajes en rojo).
1970.
Oil on canvas, 51¼ × 76¾ in. (130 × 195 cm).
Jacobo Zabludowsky Collection Mexico City.

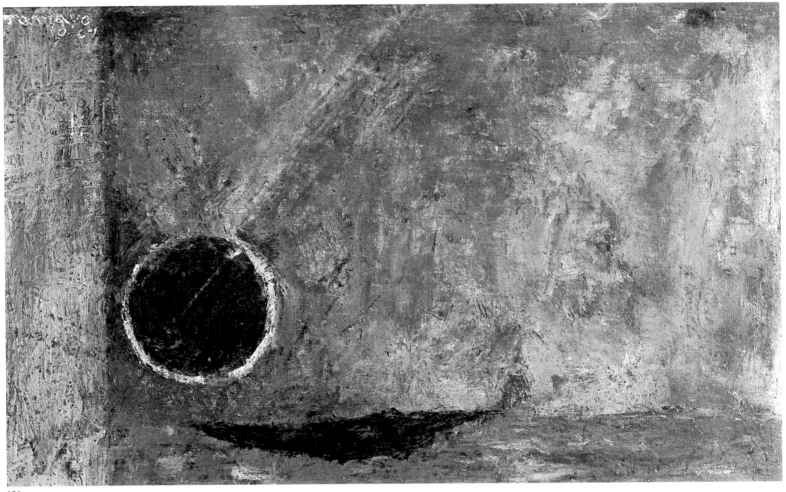

101

103

103
Man Glowing with Happiness (Hombre radiante de alegría). 1968.
Oil on canvas, 37⅜ × 51¼ in. (95 × 130 cm).
Museo de Arte Moderno/I.N.B.A., Mexico City.

104
The Man with the Bells (El hombre de los cascabeles). 1965.
Oil on canvas, 39⅜ × 31½ in. (100 × 80 cm).
Bernard Lewin Collection, Los Angeles, California.

105

106

107

105
Character (Personaje). 1968.
Oil on canvas, 31½×39⅜ in. (80×100 cm).
Bernard Lewin Collection, Los Angeles, California.

106
Pelota Players (Jugadores de pelota). 1968.
Oil on canvas, 37⅜×51¼ in. (95×130 cm).
Moisés Tanur Collection Mexico City.

107
Watermelons (Sandías). 1968.
Oil on canvas, 51¼×76¾ in. (130×195 cm).
Museo Rufino Tamayo/I.N.B.A., Mexico City.

108

108
Torsos (Torsos). 1968.
Oil on canvas, 31½ × 39⅜ in. (80 × 100 cm).
Museo de Arte Moderno/I.N.B.A., Mexico City.

109
A Man and a Woman (Un hombre y una mujer).
1969.
Oil on canvas, 39⅜ × 31½ in. (100 × 80 cm).
Abraham Zabludowsky Collection Mexico City.

109

110

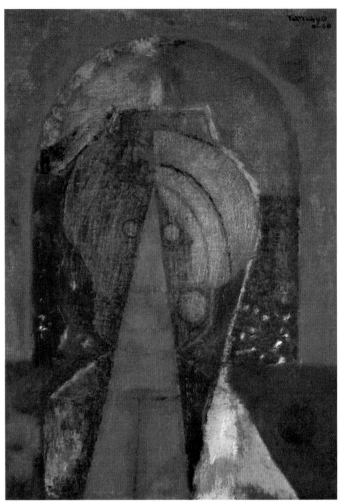

111

110
Man Sticking Out His Tongue (Hombre sacando la lengua). 1967.
Oil on canvas, 39³/₈ × 31⁷/₈ in. (100 × 81 cm).
Moisés Tanur Collection, Mexico City.

111
Head (Cabeza). 1968.
Oil on canvas, 23⁵/₈ × 15³/₄ in. (60 × 40 cm).
Orme Lewis Collection Scotland.

112

113

112
Showcase (Aparador). 1968.
Oil on canvas, 53⅛×37⅜ in. (135×95 cm).
Bernard Lewin Collection, Los Angeles, California.

113
Character in Reds and Yellows (Personaje en rojos y amarillos). 1969.
Oil on canvas, 39⅜×31½ in. (100×80 cm).
Luis Arzae Collection , Mexico City.

114
Two Children Playing (Dos niños jugando). 1967.
Oil on canvas, 53⅛ × 76¾ in. (135 × 195 cm).
Private collection, Mexico City.

115
Two Figures and the Moon (Dos figuras y la luna).
1970.
Oil on canvas, 31½ × 39⅜ in. (80 × 100 cm).
Private collection.

114

116

117

116
Torso of a Man (Torso de hombre). 1969.
Oil on canvas, 39³/₈×31¹/₂ in. (100×80 cm).
Emily Genauer Collection, New York.

117
Man in Black (Hombre en negro). 1969.
Oil on canvas, 39³/₈×31¹/₂ in. (100×80 cm).
Private collection, Mexico.

118
Head (Cabeza). 1969.
Oil on canvas, 39³/₈×33¹/₂ in. (100×85 cm).
Weinberg Collection, Chicago, Illinois.

119
Man and Woman (Hombre y mujer). 1970.
Oil on canvas, 53⅛×37⅜ in. (135×95 cm).
Peter G. Wray Collection, Phoenix, Arizona.

120
Man in Grey (Hombre en gris). 1970.
Oil on canvas, 39⅜×31½ in. (100×80 cm).
Manuel Espinosa Iglesias Collection, Mexico City.

121
Figure on a White Background (Figura sobre un fondo blanco). 1970.
Oil on canvas, 39⅜ × 31⅛ in. (100 × 79 cm).
William Link and Margery Nelson Collection, Los Angeles, California.

122
Man's torso (Torso de hombre). 1970.
Oil on canvas, 39⅜×31½ in. (100×80 cm).
Bernard Lewin Collection, Los Angeles, California.

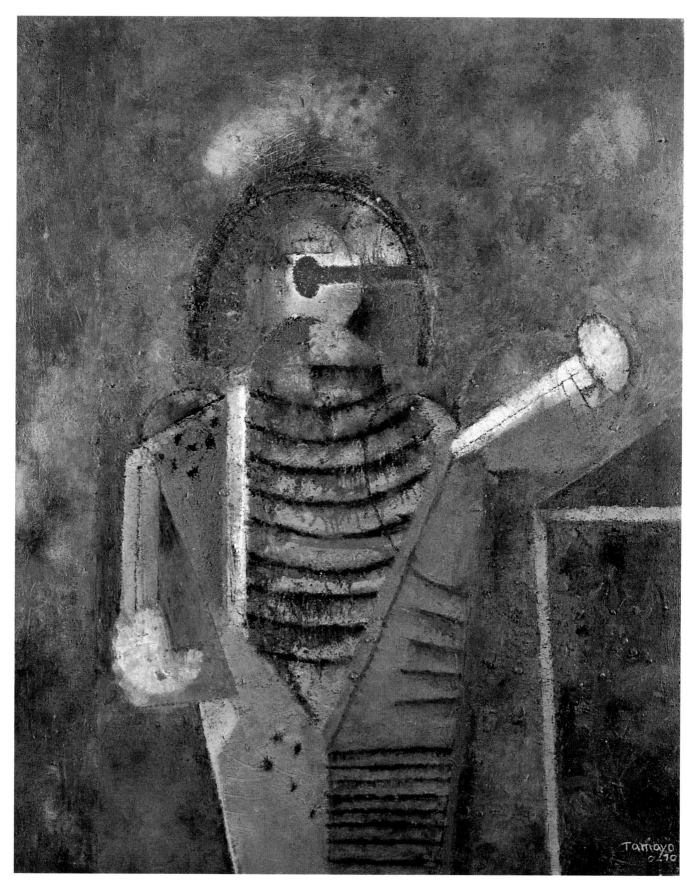

123
Floating Sphere (Esfera flotante). 1970.
Oil on canvas, 13¾ × 19¾ in. (35 × 50 cm).
Harry Weinstock Collection, New York.

124
Two Figures and the Moon (Dos figuras y la luna).
1970.
Oil on canvas, 39⅜ × 31½ in. (100 × 80 cm).
Manuel Ulloa Collection, Madrid.

Floating Sphere (Esfera flotante). 1970.
Oil on canvas, 13¾ × 19¾ in. (35 × 50 cm).
Harry Weinstock Collection, New York.

123

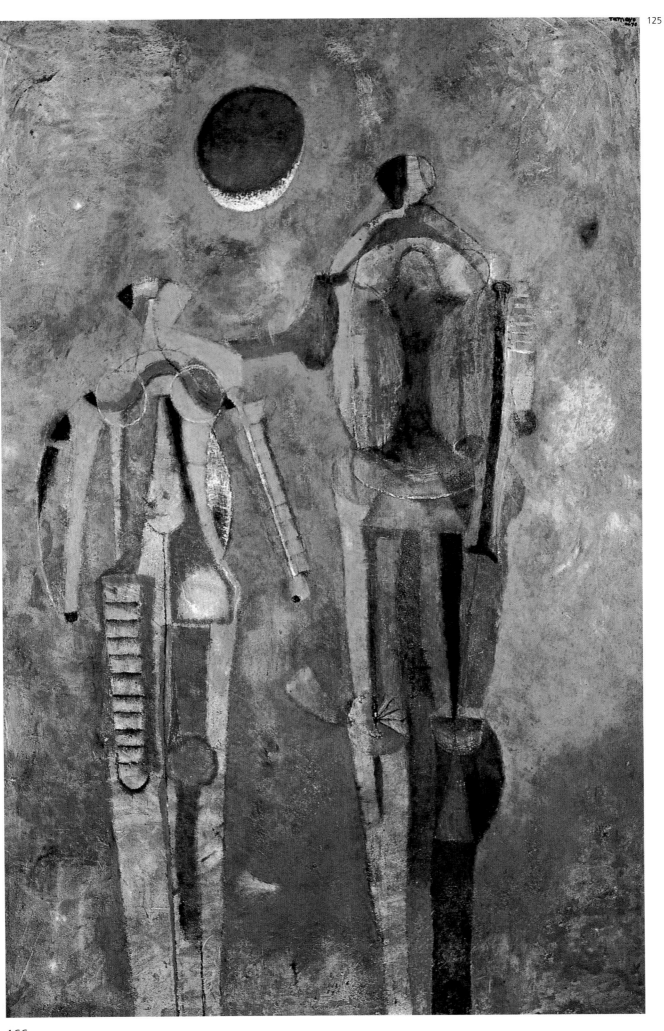

125

125
Figures (Figuras). 1970.
Oil on canvas, 76³/4×53¹/8 in.
(195×135 cm).
Luigi Bolla Collection, Milan.

126
The Loner (El solitario). 1970.
Oil on canvas, 53¹/8×37³/8 in.
(135×95 cm).
Mortimer C. Lebowitz Collecti⊘
Maclean, Virginia.

166

127

127
*Woman in Front of a Looking-Glass
(Mujer delante del espejo).* 1970.
Oil on canvas 51¼×37⅜ in.
(130×95 cm).
Museo de Arte Moderno/I.N.B.A.,
Mexico City.

128
*Character in an Interior
(Personaje en un interior).* 1970.
Oil on canvas, 51¼×37⅜ in.
(130×95 cm).
Jacobo Zabludowsky Collection,
Mexico City.

129

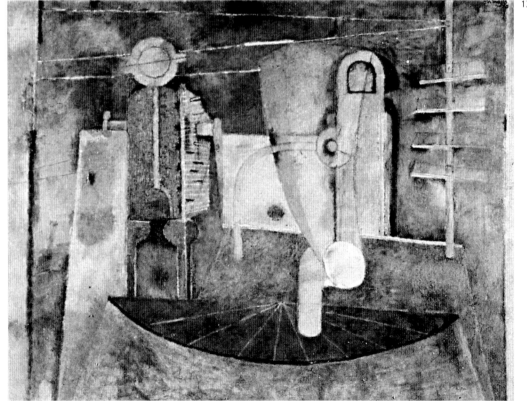

130

129
Character in Black (Personaje en negro). 1970.
Oil on canvas, 33½×43⅛ in. (85×110 cm).
Alexander Calder Collection, Saché, France.

130
Two Characters in an Interior (Dos personajes en un interior). 1970.
Oil on canvas, 38¼×51¼ in. (97×130 cm).
Leo Bakalar Collection, Boston, Massachusetts.

131
Three Characters (Tres personajes). 1970.
Oil on canvas, 39⅜×52 in. (100×132 cm).
Stewen Jacobsen Collection, New York.

131

132
Head in Red (Cabeza en rojo). 1970.
Oil on canvas, 13¾×19¾ in. (35×50 cm).
Caroline Marcuse Collection, New York.

133
Two Figures in Yellow (Dos figuras en amarillo).
1971.
Oil on canvas, 11⅞×15¾ in. (30×40 cm).
Irving Richards Collection, New York.

132

133

4
an in Red
ombre en rojo). 1970.
on canvas, 76¾ × 53⅛ in.
95 × 135 cm).
auricio Menache Collection, Mexico.

136

135
Two Women in Space (Dos mujeres en el espacio).
1970.
Oil on canvas, 51¼×38¼ in. (130×97 cm).
Sidney Berkowitz Collection, Philadelphia.

136
*Slanting Figure and Its Shadow (Figura inclinada
y su sombra).* 1971.
Oil on canvas, 33½×43¼ in. (85×110 cm).
Private Collection, Mexico.

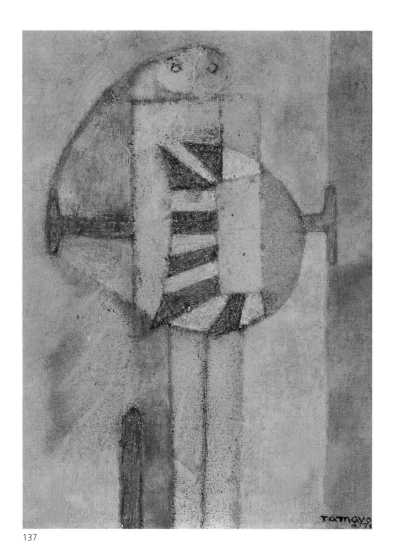

137

138

137
Man in Yellow (Hombre en amarillo). 1970.
Oil on canvas, 17¾ × 13¾ in. (45 × 35 cm).
Isaac Besudo Collection, Mexico.

138
Man and His Shadow (Hombre y su sombra). 1971
Oil on canvas, 19¾ × 15¾ in. (50 × 40 cm).
Museo de Arte Moderno/I.N.B.A., Mexico City.

139
Encounter (Reencuentro). 1972.
Oil on canvas, 53⅜ × 37⅜ in. (135 × 95 cm).
Fuji International Co. Collection, Tokyo.

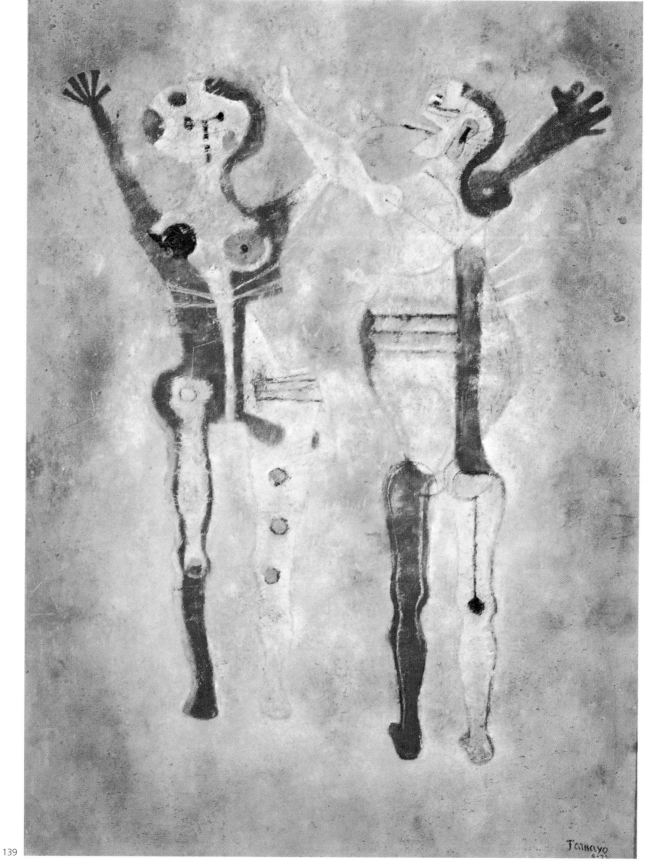

139

140

140
Family Playing (Familia jugando). 1971.
Oil on canvas, 51¼×76¾ in. (130×195 cm).
Latin American Masters Collection, Los Angeles,
California.

141
Women (Mujeres). 1971.
Oil on canvas, 53⅛×76¾ in. (135×195 cm).
Museo Rufino Tamayo/I.N.B.A., Mexico City.

141

142

143

144

142
Character (Personaje).
Oil on canvas, 13³/₄×7⁷/₈ in. (35×20 cm).
Peter G. Wray Collection Phoenix Arizona.

143
Figure in Motion (Figura en movimiento). 1971.
Oil on canvas, 15³/₄×9⁷/₈ in. (40×25 cm).
Michel Barr Collection, New York.

144
Head (Cabeza). 1971.
Oil on canvas, 13³/₄×7⁷/₈ in. (35×20 cm).
Private collection, U.S.A.

145
Man and Woman (Hombre y mujer). 1971.
Oil on canvas, 31¹/₂×27⁵/₈ in. (80×70 cm).
Norton Walbridge Collection, La Jolla.

147

146
Character (Personaje). 1972.
Oil on canvas, 39³/₈ × 31⁷/₈ in. (100 × 81 cm).
Víctor Bravo Ahuja Collection, Mexico City.

147
Figure in Red and Black (Figura en rojo y negro).
1971.
Oil on canvas, 17³/₄ × 25⁵/₈ in. (45 × 65 cm).
Winifred Breuning Collection, Oaxaca, Mexico.

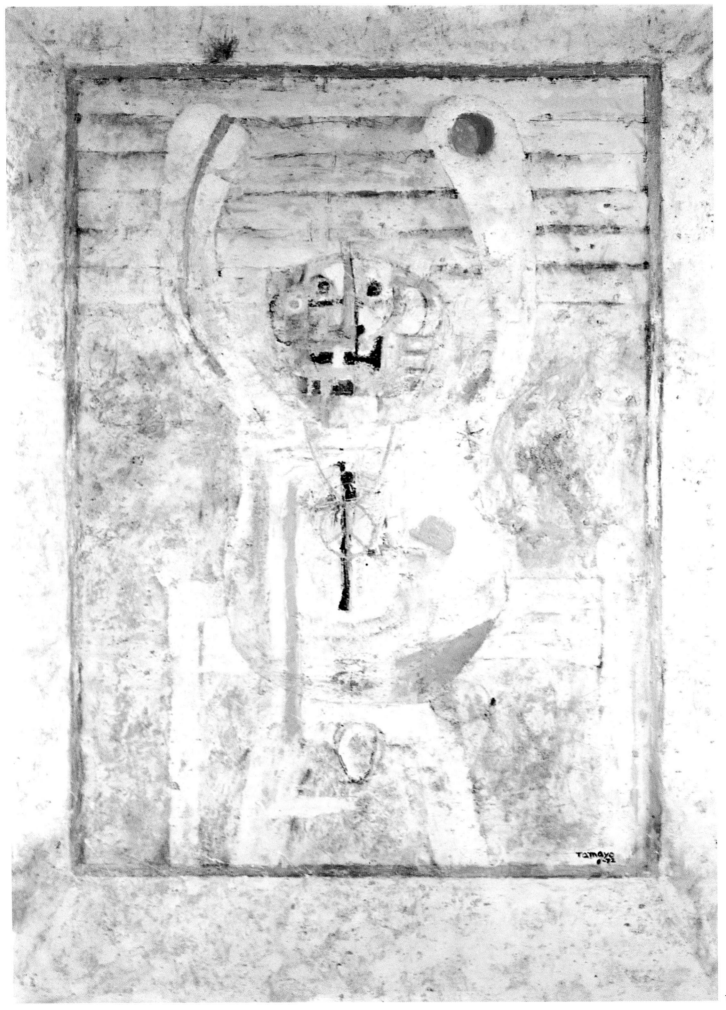

148
Hippy. 1972.
Oil on canvas, 51¼ × 37⅜ in. (130 × 95 cm).
Museo de Arte Moderno/I.N.B.A., Mexico City.

149
Portrait of Dubuffet (Retrato de Dubuffet). 1972.
Oil on canvas, 31½ × 39⅜ in. (80 × 100 cm).
Museo de Arte Moderno/I N.B.A., Mexico City.

149

150
Head in Green (Cabeza en verde). 1972.
Oil on canvas, 39⅜ × 31½ in. (100 × 80 cm).
Bernard Lewin Collection, Los Angeles, California.

151
Man's Head (Cabeza de hombre). 1972.
Oil on canvas, 39⅜×31½ in. (100×80 cm).
J. H. Sherman Collection Baltimore Maryland.

152
Eroded Landscape (Tierra erosionada). 1972.
Oil on canvas, 37⅜ × 51¼ in. (95 × 130 cm).
Armando Garza Sada Collection, Monterrey.

153
Still Life with Tankards (Bodegón jarras). 1972.
Oil on canvas, 32 × 39⅜ in. (81.2 × 100 cm).
Museo de Arte Moderno/I.N.B.A., Mexico City

152

153

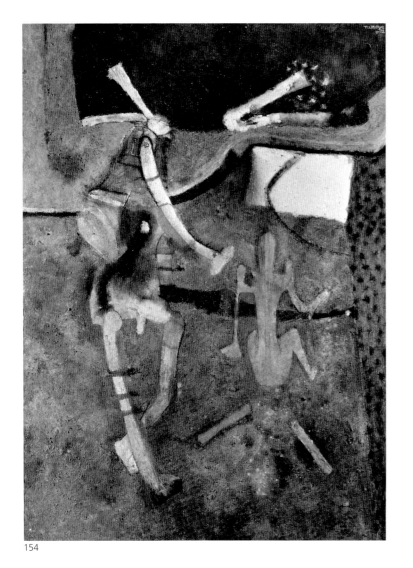

154

155

154
Dancers (Danzantes). 1972.
Oil on canvas, 53⅛ × 37⅜ in. (135 × 95 cm).
Mark Schwarz Collection Quebec.

155
Image in a Looking-Glass (Imagen en un espejo).
1972.
Oil on canvas, 39⅜ × 31½ in. (100 × 80 cm).
Kokusai Building Collection, Tokyo.

156
Study in Blue and Brown (Estudio en azul y marrón).
1973.
Oil on canvas, 57⅛ × 42½ in. (145 × 108 cm).
Bernard Lewin Collection, Los Angeles, California.

157

157
Fish Vendors (Vendedores de pescado). 1972.
Oil on canvas, 38¼×50⅜ in. (97×128 cm).
Jacob B. Noble Collection, Roslyn, New York.

158
Torso in Green (Torso en verde). 1973.
Oil on canvas, 37⅜×53⅛ in. (95×135 cm).
Lee Ault Collection, New York.

158

159

160

161

159
The Clock (El reloj). 1973.
Oil on canvas, 39⅜ × 31½ in. (100 × 80 cm).
Armando Garza Sada Collection, Monterrey.

160
Pink and Blue Head (Cabeza rosa y azul). 1972.
Oil on canvas, 15 × 9⅞ in. (38 × 25 cm).
Bernard Lewin Collection, Los Angeles, California.

161
Pink and Yellow Head (Cabeza rosa y amarilla).
1972.
Oil on canvas, 15 × 9⅞ in. (38 × 25 cm).
Bernard Lewin Collection, Los Angeles, California.

162

162
Woman in Ecstasy (Mujer en éxtasis). 1973.
Oil on canvas, 51¼×76¾ in. (130×195 cm).
Private collection.

163
Figure in Pink (Figura en rosa). 1974.
Oil on canvas, 29½×21⅝ in. (75×55 cm).
Manuel de Muga Collection, Barcelona.

164
Character (Personaje). 1973.
Oil on canvas, 31½×49¼ in. (80×125 cm).
Diego Sada Collection, Monterrey.

165
Children in Red (Niños en rojo). 1973.
Oil on canvas, 47¼×57⅛ in. (120×145 cm).
Phoenix Art Museum, Phoenix, Arizona.

164

166

167

166
Woman (Mujer). 1973.
Oil on canvas, 19¼×15¾ in. (49×40 cm).
Robert G. Rouckie Collection, Union City,
New Jersey.

167
Head (Cabeza). 1973.
Oil on canvas, 17¾×13¾ in. (45×35 cm).
J. H. Sherman Collection Baltimore Maryland.

168
Smiling Head (Cabeza que sonríe). 1973.
Oil on canvas, 14⅝×14⅝ in. (37×37 cm).
Bernard Lewin Collection, Los Angeles, California

168

169
Couple (Pareja). 1973.
Oil on canvas, 17⅞×26 in. (45.5×66 cm).
Private collection, U.S.A.

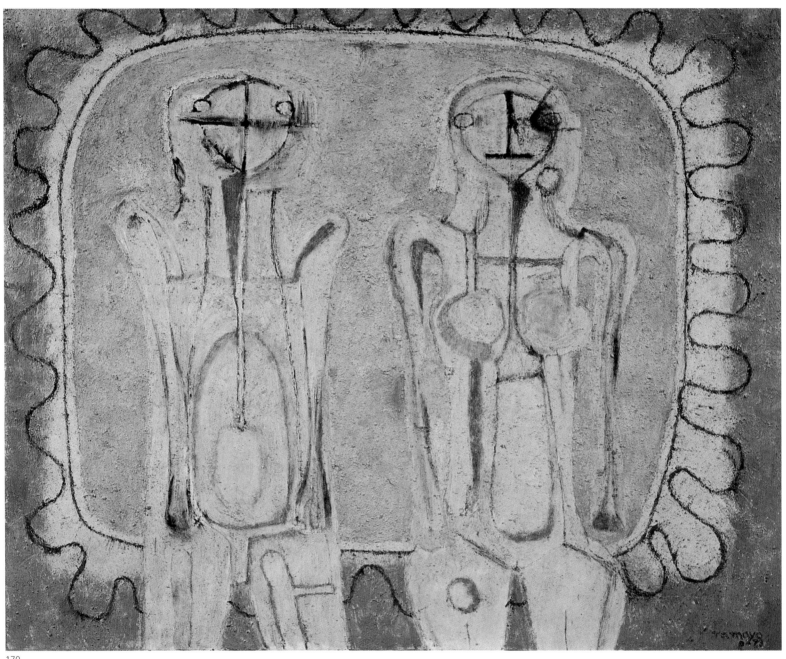

170

170
Couple (Pareja). 1973.
Oil on canvas, 31½ × 39⅜ in. (80 × 100 cm).
Harvey Amsterdam Collection, New York.

171
Man in White (Hombre en blanco). 1973.
Oil on canvas, 76¾ × 53⅛ in. (195 × 135 cm).
Márgara Garza Sada de Fernández Collection,
Monterrey.

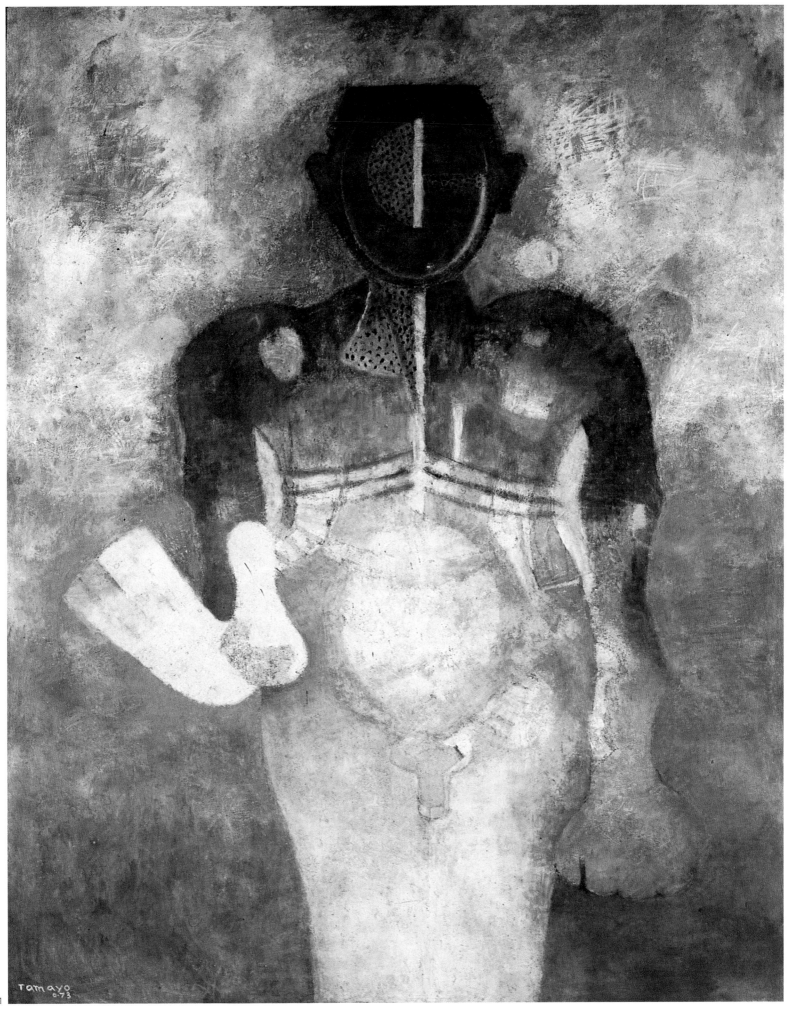

171

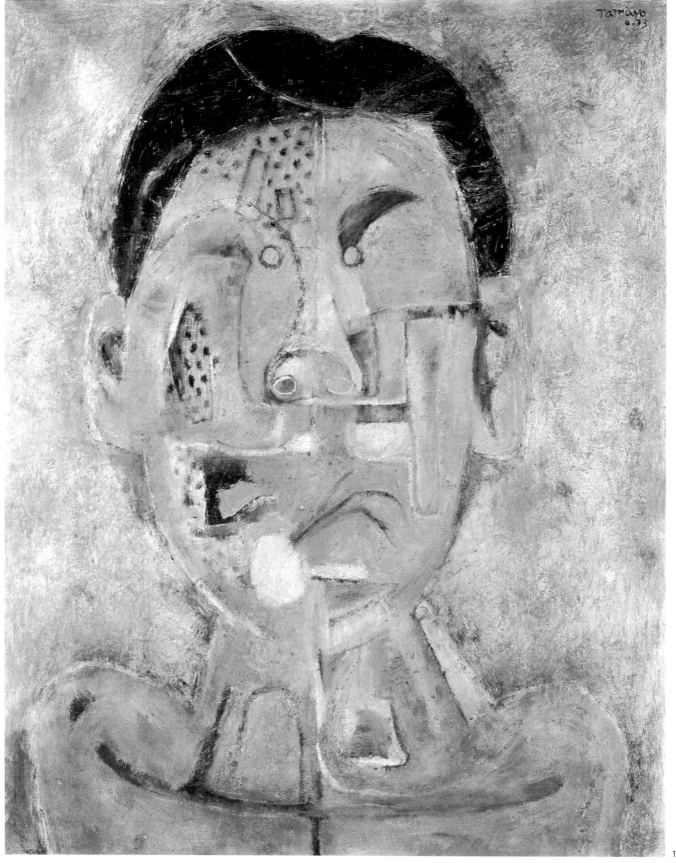

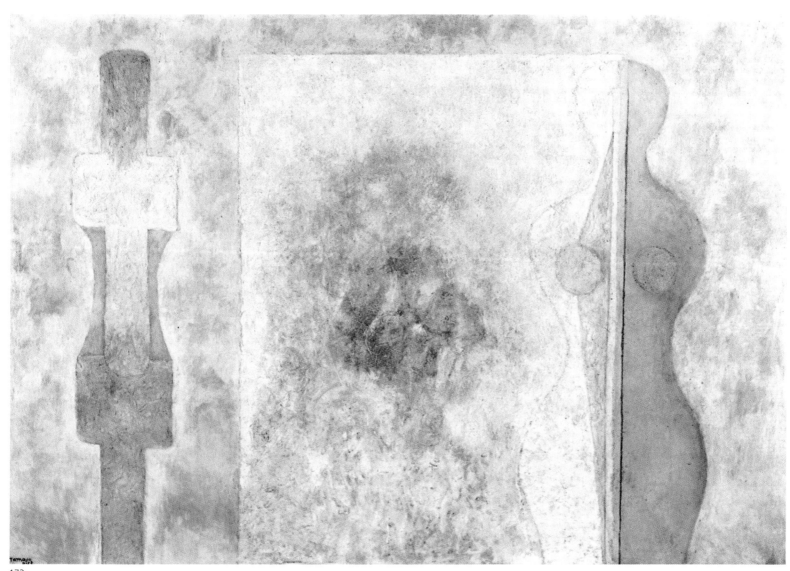

173

172
Head in Grey (Cabeza en gris). 1973.
Oil on canvas, 39³/₈ × 31⁷/₈ in. (100 × 81 cm).
Museo de Arte Moderno/I.N.B.A., Mexico City.

173
Woman Behind Glass (Mujer detrás de un vidrio)
1973.
Oil on canvas, 43¹/₄ × 59 in. (110 × 150 cm).
Private collection Mexico.

174

175

174
The Leader (El líder). 1973.
Oil on canvas, 51¼ × 38¼ in. (130 × 97 cm).
Museo de Arte Moderno/I.N.B.A., Mexico City.

175
Memorial Bust (Busto conmemorativo). 1973.
Oil on canvas, 43¼ × 59 in. (110 × 150 cm).
Gilberto Borja Navarrete, Mexico City.

177

176
Gymnasts in Pink (Gimnastas en rosa). 1974.
Oil on canvas, 59 × 51¼ in. (150 × 130 cm).
Marcos Misha Collection, Mexico City.

177
Children in a Round (Ronda de niños). 1974.
Oil on canvas, 53⅛ × 76¾ in. (135 × 195 cm).
Mimi Indaco Collection, Mexico.

179

178
High-Voltage Pylon
(Torre de alta tensión). 1974.
Oil on canvas, 76¾ × 51¼ in.
(195 × 130 cm).
Olga Tamayo Collection, Mexico City.

179
Construction
(Construcción). 1974.
Oil on canvas 76¾ × 51¼ in.
(195 × 130 cm).
Galerie de France, Paris.

180
Blocked Road
(Camino cerrado). 1974.
Oil on canvas, 27⅝ × 43¼ in.
(70 × 110 cm).
Olga Tamayo Collection, Mexico City.

180

181
The Comedians (Los comediantes). 1974.
Oil on canvas, 37⅜×51¾ in. (95×130 cm).
Armando Garza Sada Collection Monterrey.

182
Carnival (Carnavalesca). 1974.
Oil on canvas, 76¾×51¼ in. (195×130 cm).
Bernardo Garza Sada Collection Monterrey.

181

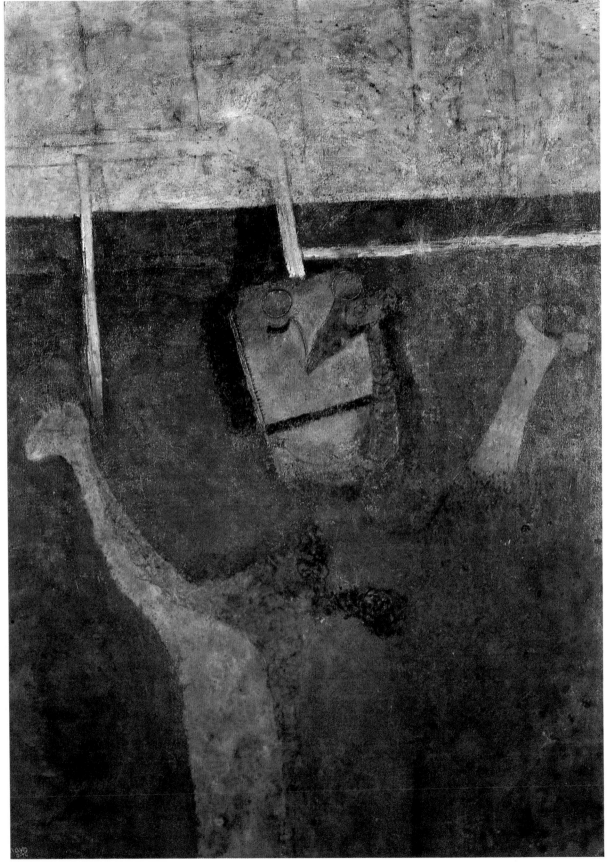

184

183
Character (Personaje). 1974.
Oil on canvas, 51¼×37⅜ in. (130×95 cm).
Private collection.

184
The Juggler (El juglar). 1974.
Oil on canvas, 45¼×55⅛ in. (115×140 cm).
Mary-Anne Martin Collection, New York.

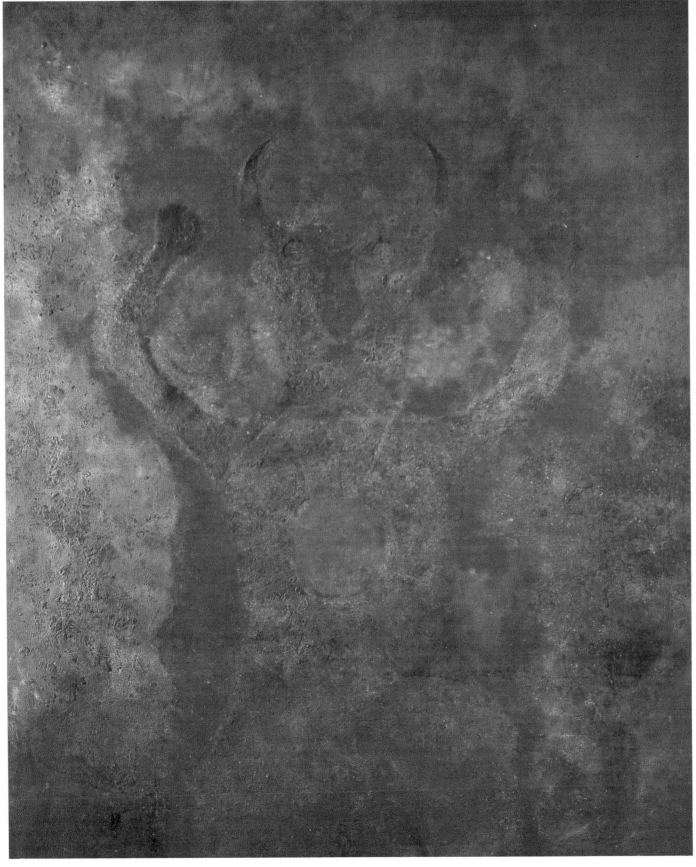

186

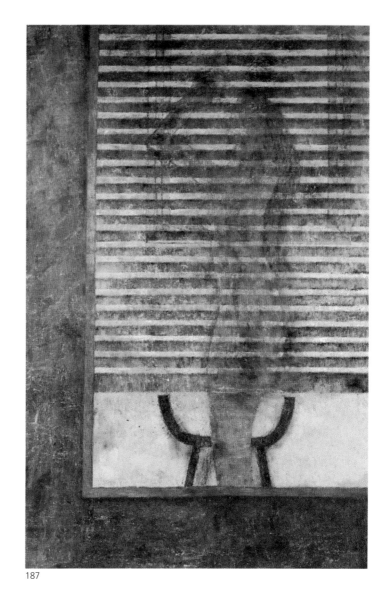

187

185
Portrait of the Devil (Retrato del diablo). 1974.
Oil on canvas, 55⅛×45¼ in. (140×115 cm).
Víctor Bravo Ahuja Collection, Mexico City.

186
Blonde Woman (Mujer rubia). 1974.
Oil on canvas, 76¾×51¼ in. (195×130 cm).
Galerie de France, Paris.

187
The Indiscreet Window (La ventana indiscreta).
1974.
Oil on canvas, 76¾×51¼ in. (195×130 cm).
Galerie de France, Paris.

188
The Beach (La playa). 1974.
Oil on canvas, 43¼×49¼ in. (110×125 cm).
Márgara Garza Sada de Fernández Collection
Monterrey.

189
Arid Landscape (Paisaje árido). 1974.
Oil on canvas, 53⅛×63 in. (135×160 cm).
Armando Garza Sada Collection Monterrey.

190
Show Dog (Perro de exposición). 1974.
Oil on canvas, 53⅛×76¾ in. (135×195 cm).
Museo de Arte Moderno Caracas.

188

189

190

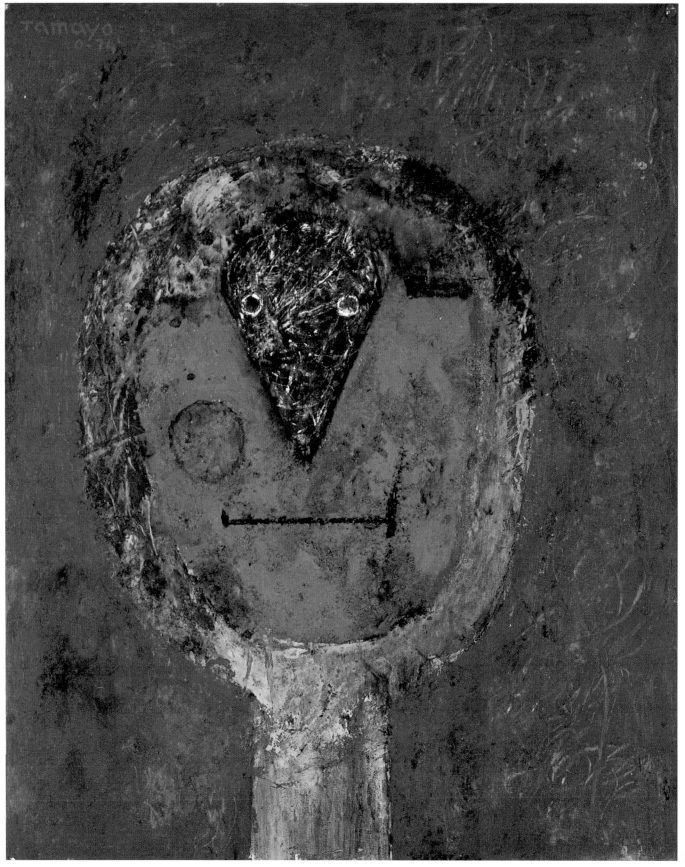

192

191
Head (Cabeza). 1974.
Oil on canvas, 18½×15 in. (47×38 cm).
Alinka Zabludowsky Collection, Mexico City.

192
Dialogues (Diálogos). 1974.
Oil on canvas, 53⅛×76¾ in. (135×195 cm).
Bernard Lewin Collection, Los Angeles, California.

193
Head in White (Cabeza en blanco). 1975.
Oil on canvas, 31½ × 39⅜ in. (80 × 100 cm).
Armando Garza Sada Collection Monterrey.

194
Figure in White (Figura en blanco). 1975.
Oil on canvas, 51¼ × 37⅜ in. (130 × 95 cm).
Jacobo Zabludowsky Collection, Mexico City.

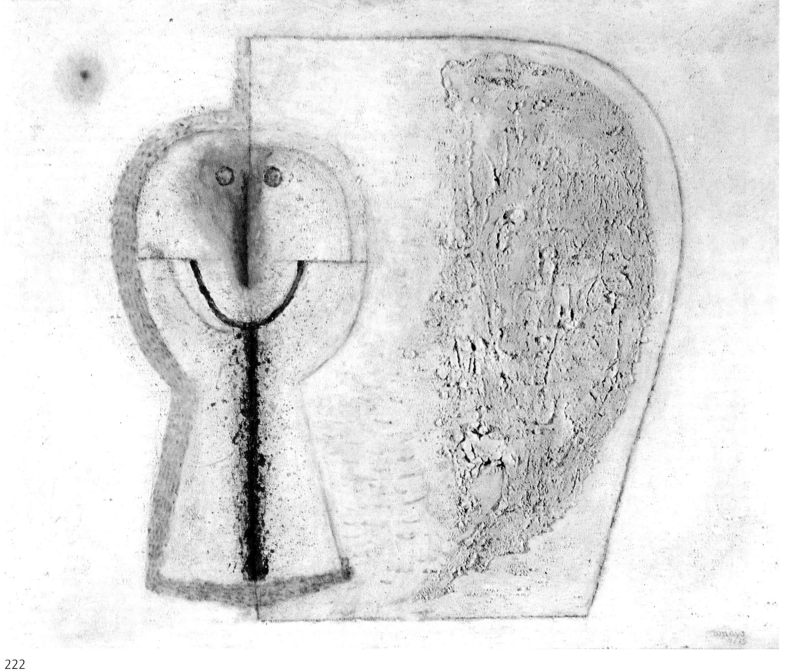

193

194

195

195
Man with His Arms Raised (Hombre con brazos en alto). 1975.
Acrylic on canvas, 38¼ × 51¼ in. (97 × 130 cm).
Private collection, Mexico.

196
The Twins (Las gemelas). 1975.
Oil on canvas, 57⅛ × 43¼ in. (145 × 110 cm).
Silvia Ripstein Collection, New York.

198

197
The Shout (El grito). 1975.
Oil on canvas, 51¼×37⅜ in. (130×95 cm).
Jacobo Zabludowsky Collection, Mexico City.

198
Double Portrait (Doble retrato). 1975.
Acrylic on canvas, 33½×39⅜ in. (85×100 cm).
Gilberto Borja Collection, Mexico City.

227

199

200

199
Striped Figure (Figura rayada). 1975.
Oil on canvas, 51¼×38¼ in. (130×97 cm).
Museum of Modern Art, Tokyo.

200
Two figures (Dos figuras). 1975.
Acrylic on canvas, 51¼×38¼ in. (130×97 cm).
Private collection, Mexico.

201

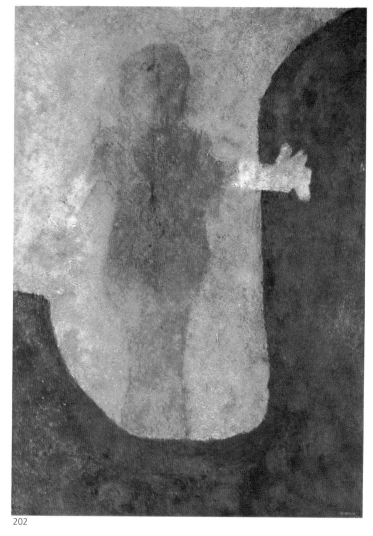

202

201
Woman and Her Ghost (Mujer y su fantasma).
1975.
Oil on canvas, 68⁷⁄₈×55⅛ in. (175×140 cm).
Private collection, Mexico City.

202
Character in Red (Personaje en rojo). 1975.
Acrylic on canvas, 51¼×38¼ in. (130×97 cm).
Private collection.

203

203
Dialogue (Diálogo). 1975.
Oil on canvas, 43¼×57⅜ in. (110×145 cm).
Jacobo Zabludowsky Collection, Mexico City.

204
Man in Red and Green (Hombre en rojo y verde).
1975.
Oil on canvas, 51¼×37⅜ in. (130×95 cm).
José Pintado Collection, Mexico City.

205

205
Man Beside a Wall (Hombre junto a un muro).
1975.
Oil on canvas, 37³/₈×51¼ in. (95×130 cm).
Robert and Avy Miller Collection, Encino, California.

206
The Red Hand (La mano roja). 1975.
Acrylic on canvas, 37³/₈×51¼ in. (95×130 cm).
Jacobo Zabludowsky Collection, Mexico City.

206

208

207
*Man Close to the Window (Hombre cerca
de la ventana).* 1975.
Oil on canvas, 51¼ × 37⅜ in. (130 × 95 cm).
Neda Anhalt Collection, Mexico City.

208
The Green Door (La puerta verde). 1975.
Acrylic on canvas, 39⅜ × 59 in. (100 × 150 cm).
Jacobo Zabludowsky Collection, Mexico City.

209

210

211

209
Emergent Man (Hombre emergente). 1975.
Oil on canvas, 31½ × 39⅜ in. (80 × 100 cm).
Museo de Bellas Artes, Caracas.

210
Still Life (Bodegón). 1976.
Oil on canvas, 31⅞ × 39⅜ in. (81 × 100 cm).
Armando Garza Sada Collection, Monterrey.

211
Boy in Red (Niño en rojo). 1975.
Oil on canvas, 38¼ × 53⅛ in. (97 × 135 cm).
Private collection, U.S.A.

213

212
*Monumental to an Unknown Hero (Monumento a
un héroe desconocido).* 1975.
Oil on canvas, 51³/₄×38¹/₄ in. (130×97 cm).
Private collection, Los Angeles, California.

213
Still Life (Bodegón). 1975.
Oil on canvas, 31⁷/₈×39³/₈ in. (81×100 cm).
Anna Bonomi Collection, Milan.

214

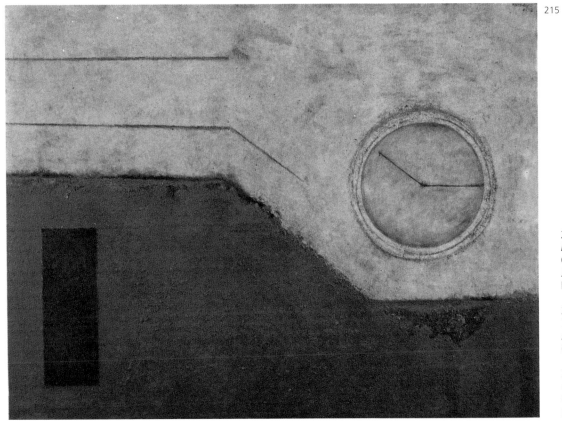

215

214
Landscape in Grey (Paisaje en gris). 1975.
Oil on canvas, 23⅝ × 33½ in. (60 × 85 cm).
Jacobo Zabludowsky Collection,
Mexico City.

215
The Forgotten Clock (El reloj olvidado). 1975.
Acrylic on canvas, 38¼ × 51¼ in. (97 × 130 cm).
Olga Tamayo Collection, Mexico City.

216
Character in Green (Personaje en verde). 1975.
Oil on canvas, 39⅜ × 31½ in. (100 × 80 cm).
Neda Anhalt Collection, Mexico City.

217

217
Two Figures (Dos figuras). 1975.
Oil on canvas, 53⅛ × 76¾ in. (135 × 195 cm).
Anna Bonomi Collection, Milan.

218
Boy in Red (Niño en rojo). 1976.
Oil on canvas, 51¼ × 38¼ in. (130 × 97 cm).
Private collection, Mexico.

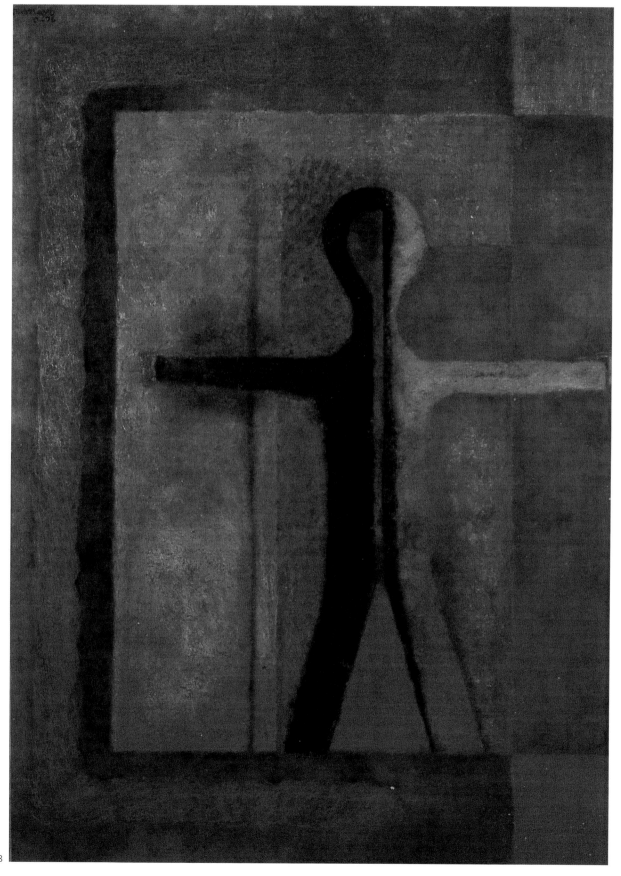

219

219
Still Life (Naturaleza muerta). 1976.
Oil on canvas, 31½ × 39⅜ in. (80 × 100 cm).
Arnaldo Pomodoro Collection, Milan.

220
Arrangement (Arreglo). 1976.
Oil on canvas, 51¼ × 38¼ in. (130 × 97 cm).
Private collection, New York.

222

221
*Woman in White
(Mujer en blanco)*. 1976.
Oil on canvas, 39³/₈×31¹/₂ in.
(100×80 cm).
Alberto Sánchez Palazuelos
Collection .

222
*Man in Red
(Hombre en rojo)*. 1976.
Oil *on* canvas 51¹/₄×38⁵/₈ in.
(130×98 cm).
Museo Rufino Tamayo/I.N.B.A.,
Mexico City.

223

224

223
Hippy Woman (Mujer hippy). 1976.
Oil on canvas, 51¼×38¼ in. (130×97 cm).
Private collection, Mexico.

224
Still Life with Fruit Bowl (Bodegón con frutero).
1976.
Oil on canvas, 38¼×51¾ in. (97×130 cm).
Rómulo Betancourt Collection, Caracas.

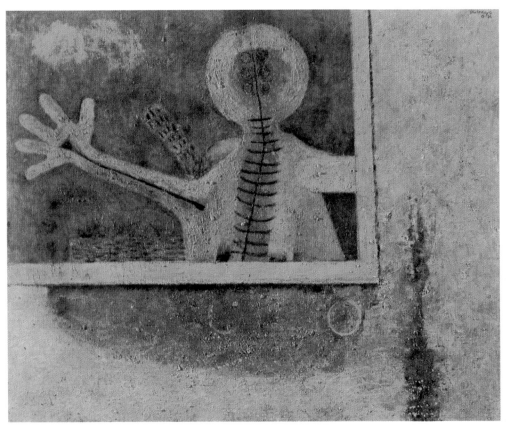

225

226

225
Man at the Window (Hombre en la ventana). 1976.
Oil on canvas, 31½ × 39⅜ in. (80 × 100 cm).
Private collection, Brazil.

226
Pile of Plates (Pila de platos). 1977.
Oil on canvas, 31⅞ × 39⅜ in. (81 × 100 cm).
Private collection, New York.

227
Man (Hombre). 1976.
Oil on canvas, 51¼ × 38¼ in. (130 × 97 cm).
Mauricio Berger Collection.

250

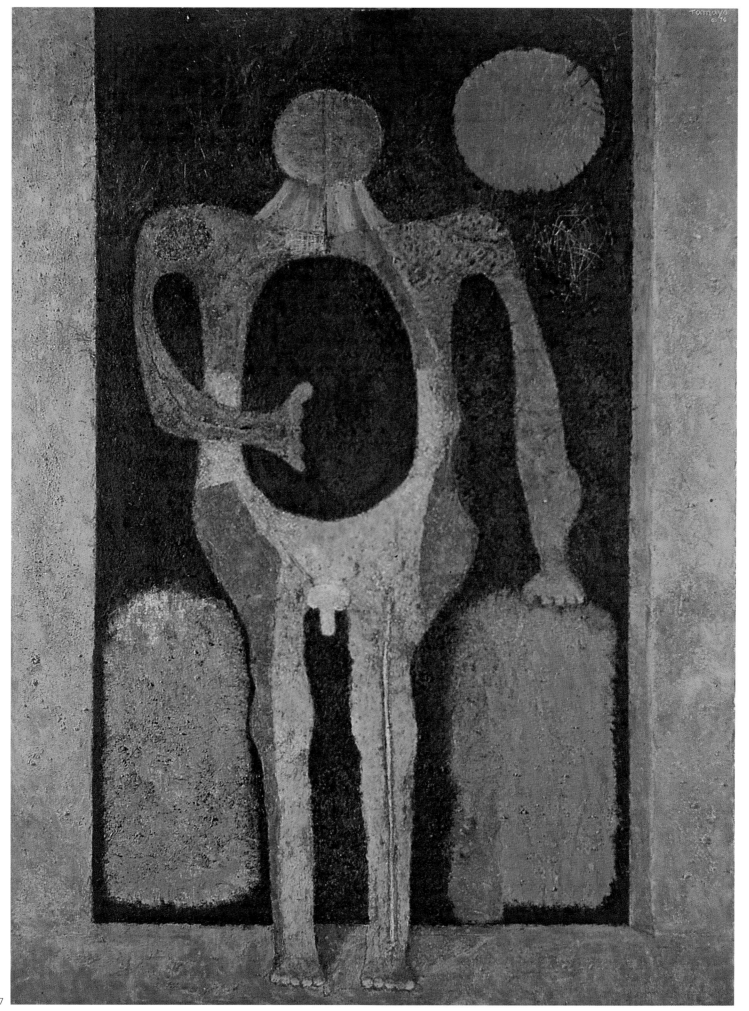

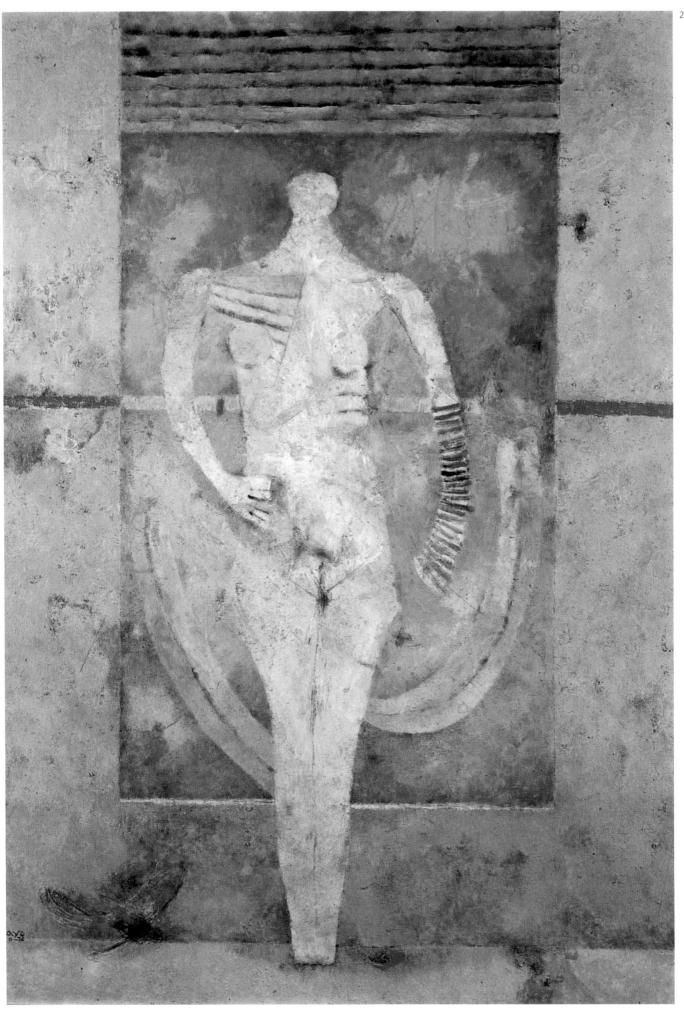

228
Nude in White
(Desnudo en blanco). 1976
Oil on canvas, 76¾×53⅛
(195×135 cm).
Museo Rufino Tamayo/I.N.
Mexico City.

229
Empty Fruit Bowl
(Frutero vacío). 1976.
Oil on canvas, 59×43½ ir
(150×110.5 cm).
Galería Arvil, Mexico City.

230
Woman in a Cave (Mujer en una cueva). 1977.
Oil on canvas, 53⅛×39⅜ in. (135×100 cm).
Alinka Zabludowsky Collection, Mexico City.

231
Pregnant Woman (Mujer embarazada). 1976.
Oil on canvas, 39⅜×31⅞ in. (100×81 cm).
Lucha Villa Collection, Mexico City.

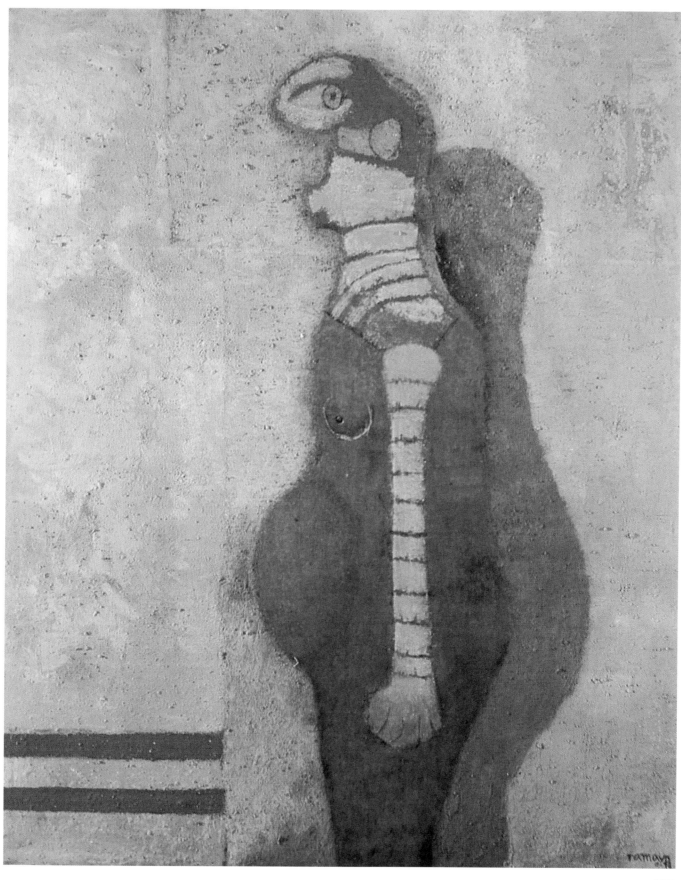

232

232
The Great Galaxy (La gran galaxia). 1978.
Oil on canvas, 38¼ × 54¼ in. (97 × 137.8 cm).
Museo Rufino Tamayo/I.N.B.A., Mexico City.

233
Aerial Space (Espacio aéreo). 1977.
Oil on canvas, 39⅜ × 31⅞ in. (100 × 81 cm).
Private collection, Mexico.

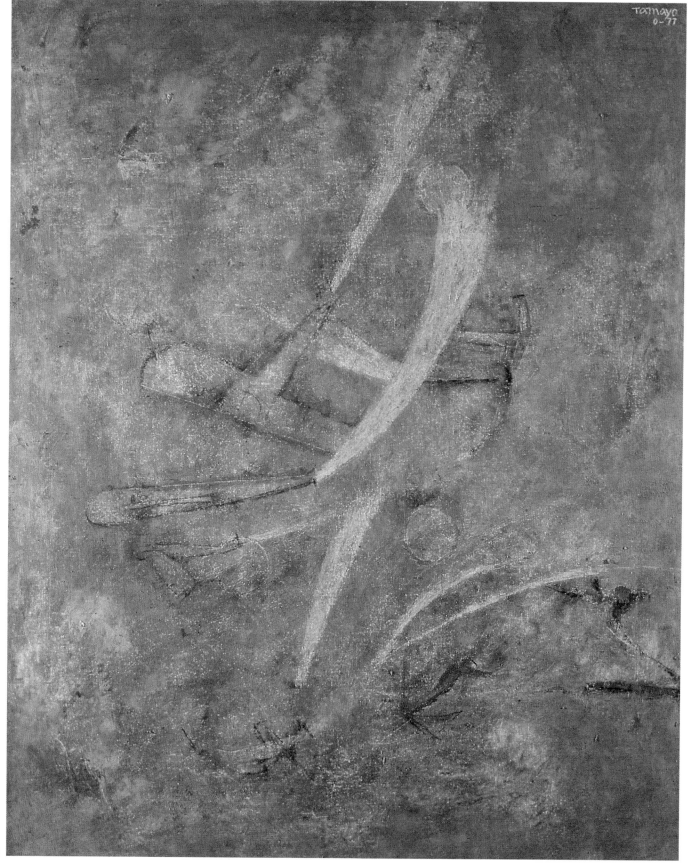

Tamayo 234

235

234
Dancer (Danzante). 1977.
Oil on canvas, 68½ × 54¾ in. (174 × 139 cm).
The Solomon R. Guggenheim Museum, New York.

235
*Two Men in a Landscape (Dos hombres
en un paisaje)*. 1977.
Oil on canvas, 38 × 51½ in. (96.5 × 130.8 cm).
Private collection, Mexico.

236

236
Man with His Hands Clasped
(Hombre con las manos cruzadas). 1978
Oil on canvas, 53⅛×37⅜ in.
(135×95 cm).
Mme Susan Lloyd Collection, Paris.

237
Waning Moon
(Cuarto menguante). 1978.
Acrylic on canvas, 76¾×53⅛ in.
(195×135 cm).
Private collection U.S.A.

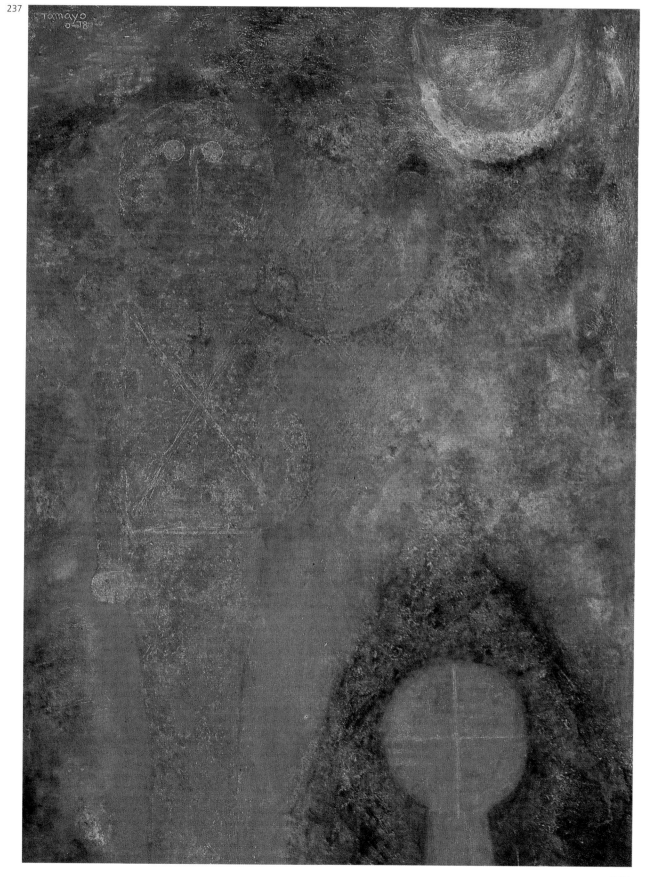

238

238
Man with Crossed Arms (Hombre con los brazos cruzados). 1978.
Oil on canvas, 38¼×51¼ in. (97×130 cm).
Private collection, Mexico City.

239
Two Figures on a Purple Background (Dos figuras sobre fondo morado). 1978.
Oil on canvas, 53⅛×37⅜ in. (135×95 cm).
Gian Franco Arnoldi Collection.

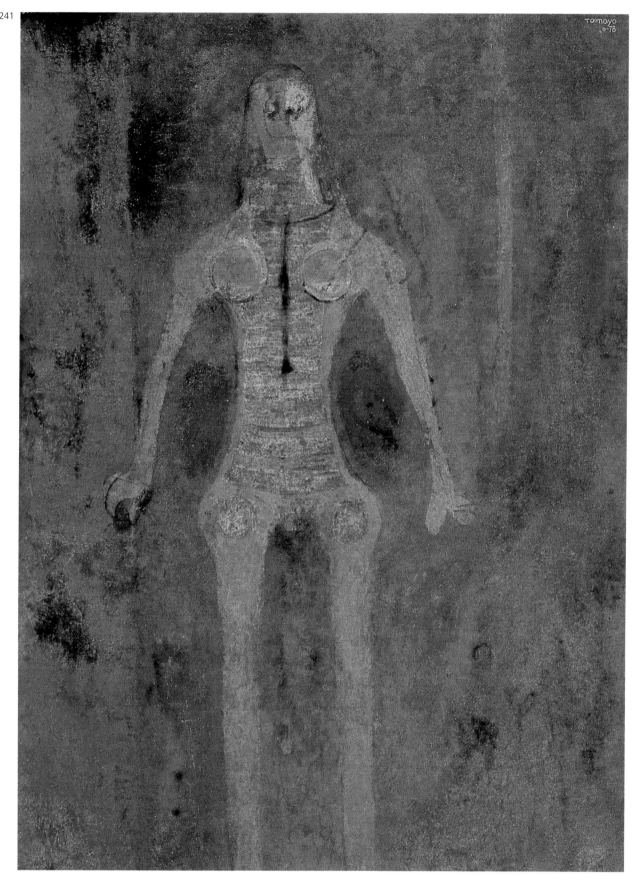

241

240
Red Head (Cabeza roja). 1978.
Oil on canvas, 39³/₈×31¹/₂ in.
(100×80 cm).
Mme Susan Lloyd Collection, Paris.

241
Standing Woman (mujer de pie). 1978.
Oil on canvas, 59×43¹/₄ in.
(150×110 cm).
Private collection, Mexico.

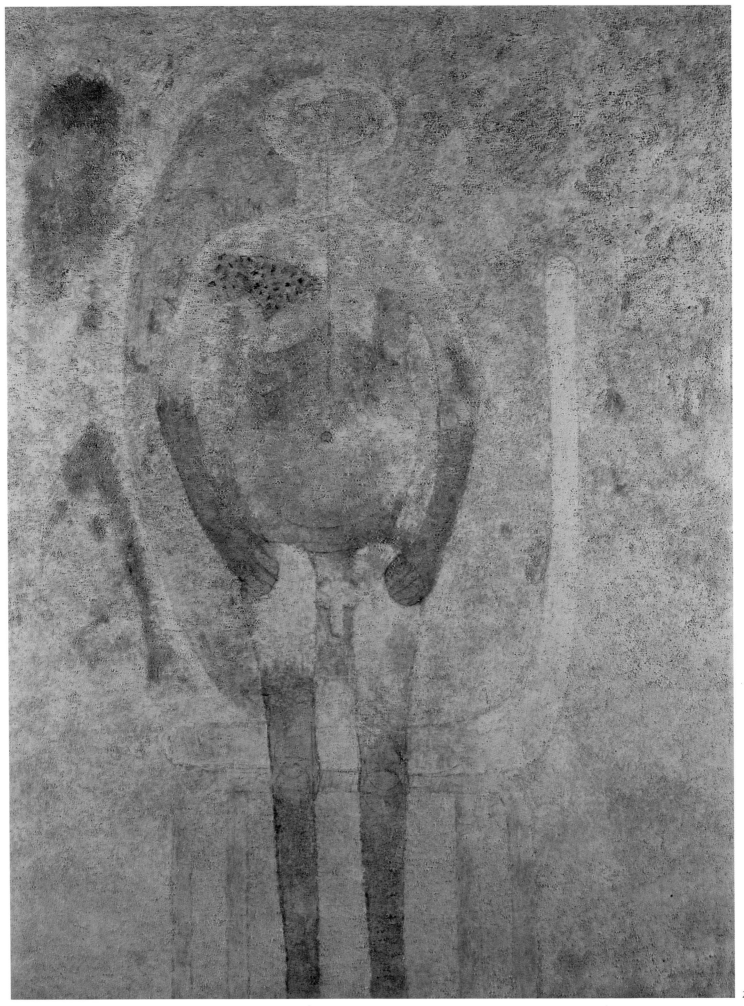

242
Figure in White and Yellow (Figura en blanco y amarillo). 1978.
Oil on canvas, 53⅛ × 43¼ in. (135 × 110 cm).
Private collection, Mexico.

243
Man at the Door (Hombre a la puerta). 1978.
Oil on canvas, 43¼ × 53⅛ in. (110 × 135 cm).
Private collection, U.S.A.

243

244

245

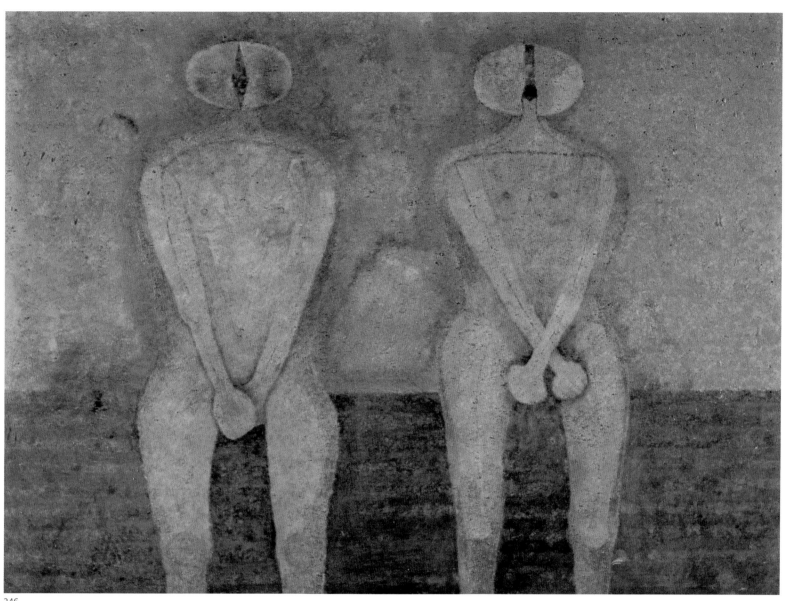

246

244
Torso (Torso). 1978.
Oil on canvas, 31¹/₂×39³/₈ in. (80×100 cm).
David Somerset Collection, London.

245
Ghost at the Door (Fantasma a la puenta). 1978.
Oil on canvas, 38¹/₄×51¹/₄ in. (97×130 cm).
Bernard Lewin Collection, Los Angeles, California.

246
Two Women (Dos mujeres). 1979.
37³/₈×51¹/₄ in. (95×130 cm).
Private collection, Caracas.

247
*Woman Smiling
(Mujer sonriente)*. 1979.
Oil on canvas, 51¼×37⅜ in.
(130×95 cm).
Private collection, U.S.A.

248
Acrobat (Saltimbanqui). 1979.
Oil on canvas, 53⅛×37⅜ in.
(135×95 cm).
Bernard Lewin Collection,
Los Angeles, California.

249

249
Man (Hombre). 1979.
Acrylic on canvas, 51¼ × 37⅜ in. (130 × 95 cm).
Bernard Lewin Collection, Los Angeles, California.

250
Man (Personaje). 1979.
Acrylic on canvas, 76¾ × 51¼ in. (195 × 130 cm).
Mr and Mrs Stephen Jacobson Collection.

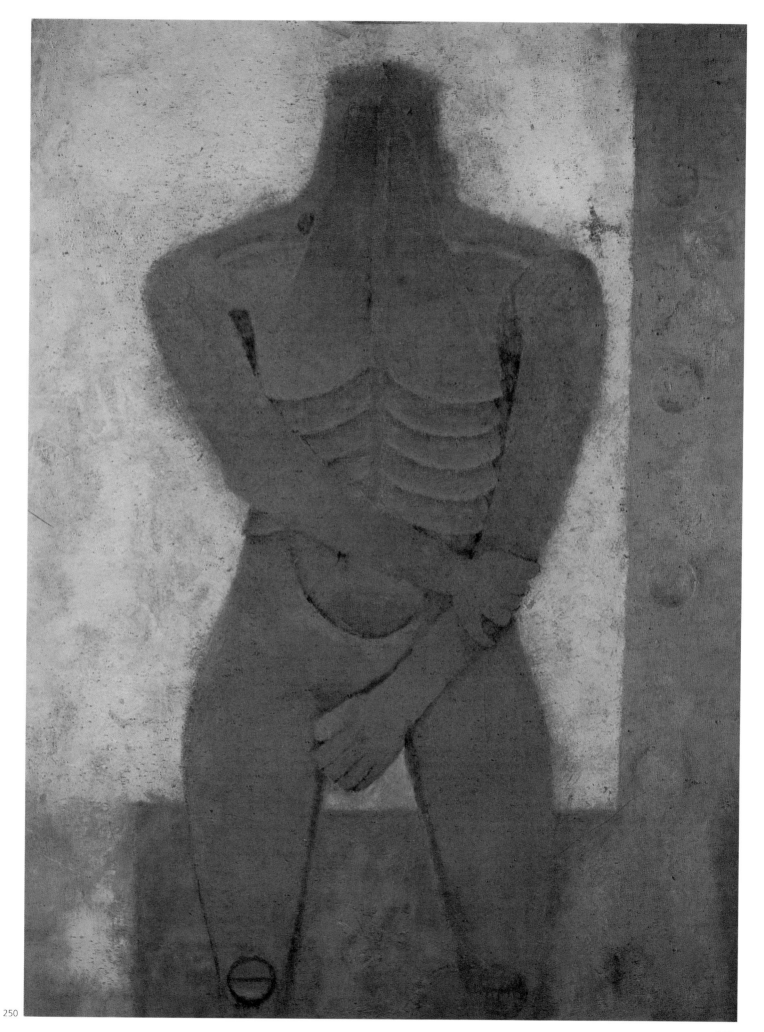

251
Man and His Ghost
(Hombre y su fantasma). 1980.
Oil on canvas, 59×43¼ in.
(150×110 cm).
Industrias Resistol Collection, Mexico.

252
Dancer (Danzante). 1980.
Acrylic on canvas, 51¼×37⅜ in.
(130×95 cm).
Museo Rufino Tamayo/I.N.B.A.,
Mexico City.

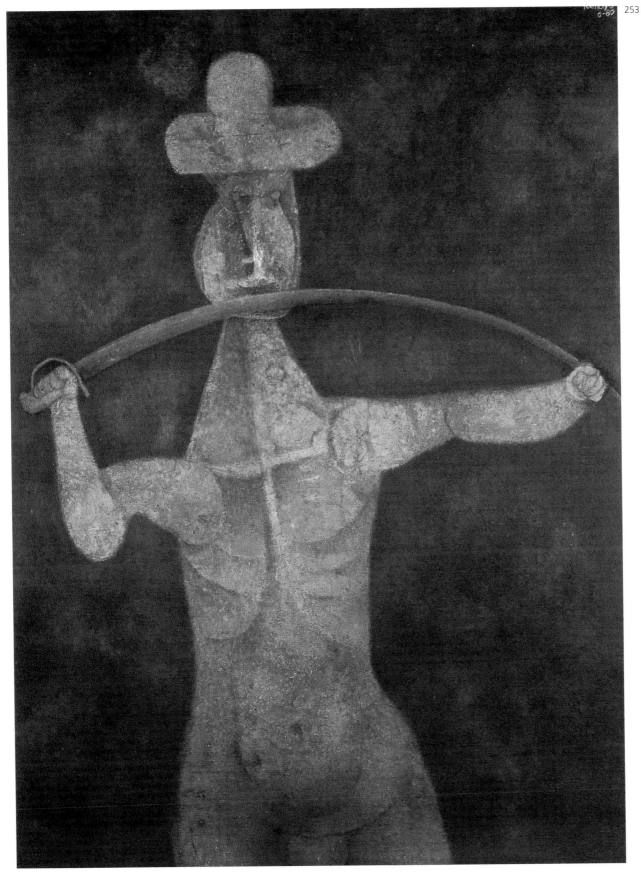

253

254

253
The Man with the Sabre
(El hombre del sable).
1980.
Acrylic on canvas, 51¼ × 37⅜ in.
(130 × 95 cm).
Claude Terrain Collection, Mexico City.

254
Man (Hombre). 1979.
Acrylic on canvas, 51¼ × 37⅜ in.
(130 × 95 cm).
Private collection.

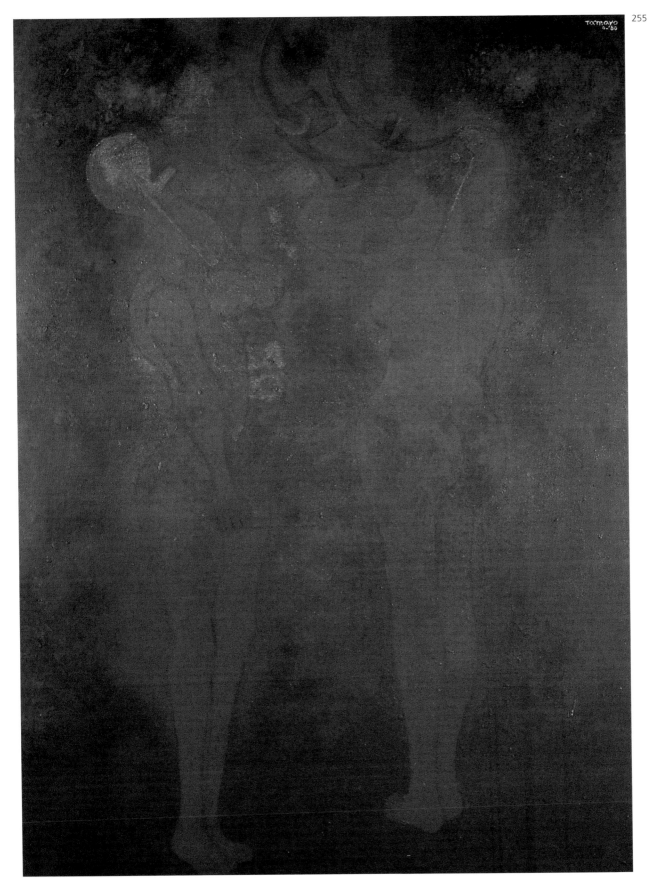

256

255
Friends of the Birds
(Amigas de los pájaros). 1980.
Oil on canvas, 51¼×37⅜ in.
(130×95 cm).
Grupo Industrial Alfa Collection,
Monterrey.

256
Shout (Grito). 1980.
Acrylic on canvas, 51¼×37⅜ in.
(130×95 cm).

257
Man Attacked by a Bird (Hombre atacado por un pájaro). 1980.
Acrylic on canvas, 51 × 38 in. (129.5 × 96.5 cm).
Esthela Santos Collection, Monterrey.

258
Men Walking (Hombres caminando). 1980.
Oil on canvas, 51 × 37 in. (129.5 × 94 cm).
Mr Tony Randall Collection, New York.

260

259
Boy with Cap (Niño con cachucha). 1980.
Oil on canvas, 39½ × 31⅜ in. (100.3 × 79.7 cm).

260
Character in an Interior (Personaje en un interior).
1981.
Oil on canvas, 31½ × 49¼ in. (80 × 125 cm).
Marlborough Gallery, New York.

261

261
Man and Woman (Hombre y mujer). 1981.
Oil on canvas, 37³/₈ × 53¹/₈ in. (95 × 135 cm).

262
Three Characters Singing (Tres personajes cantando).
1981.
Oil on canvas, 37³/₈ × 53¹/₈ in. (95 × 135 cm).
Private collection, Mexico.

262

263
Two Characters (Dos personajes). 1981.
Oil on canvas, 37⅜ × 53⅜ in. (95 × 135 cm).

264
Couple on the Terrace (Pareja en la terraza). 1981.
Oil on *canvas,* 51 × 71 in. (129.5 × 180.4 cm).
Latin American Masters Gallery, Beverly Hills,
California.

263

265
Man and Woman (Hombre y mujer). 1981.
Oil on canvas, 49⅛×70⅞ in. (124.8×180 cm).
Tate Gallery London.

266
Red Torso (Torso rojo). 1981.
Oil on canvas 70⅞×49¼ in. (180×125 cm).
Bernard Lewin Collection, Los Angeles, California.

265

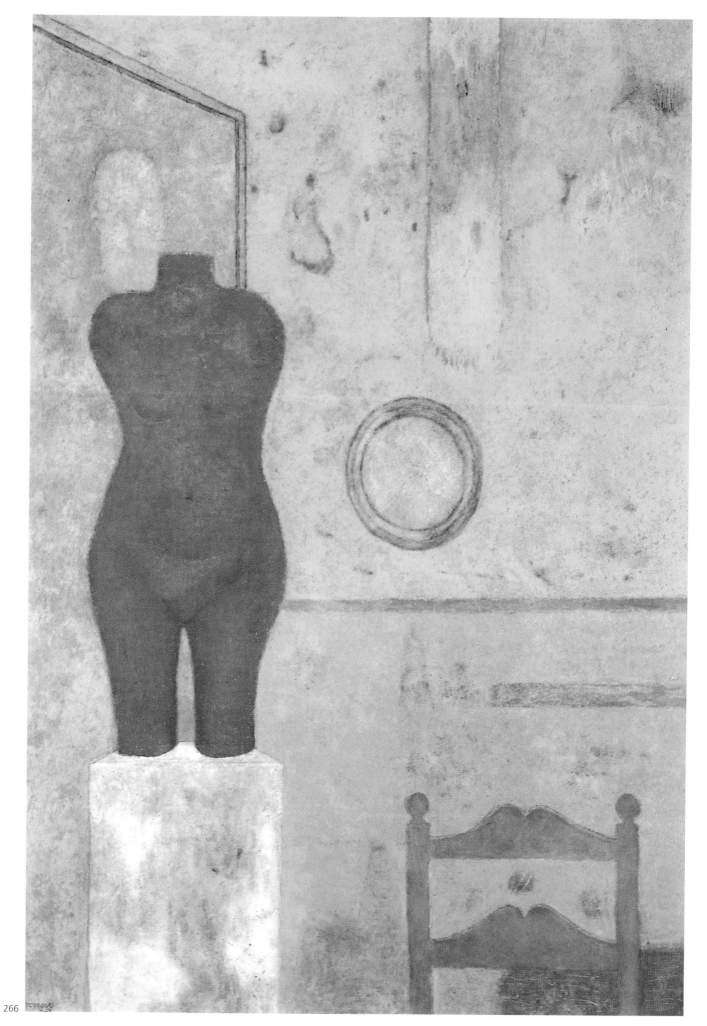

268

267
Nude Man (Desnudo de hombre). 1982.
Oil on canvas, 51¼ × 37⅜ in. (130 × 95 cm).
Bernardo and Irma Zarkin Collection, Mexico City.

268
Forgotten Clock (Reloj olvidado). 1986.
Oil on canvas, 38¼ × 51¼ in. (97 × 130 cm).
Olga Tamayo Collection, Mexico City.

269

269
The Family (La familia). 1987.
Oil on canvas, 53⅛×76¾ in. (135×195 cm).
Olga Tamayo Collection, Mexico City.

270
Offering of Fruits (Ofrenda de frutas). 1987.
Oil on canvas, 55⅛×68⅞ in. (140×175 cm).
Private collection, Mexico City.

270

271

271
The Three Friends (Los tres amigos). 1987.
Oil on canvas, 43¼×59⅞ in. (110×152 cm).
Marlborough Gallery Collection, New York, N.Y.

272
Today (Hoy). 1988.
Oil on canvas, 51¼×76¾ in. (130×195 cm).
Olga Tamayo Collection, Mexico City.

272

273

273
Bathers in Cancún (Bañistas en Cancún). 1988.
Oil on canvas, 37³/₈ × 51¹/₄ in. (95 × 130 cm).
Private collection, Mexico City.

274
Hands Up (Manos arriba). 1989.
Oil on canvas, 37³/₈ × 51¹/₄ in. (95 × 130 cm).
Latin American Masters Collection, Los Angeles,
California.

274

275

276

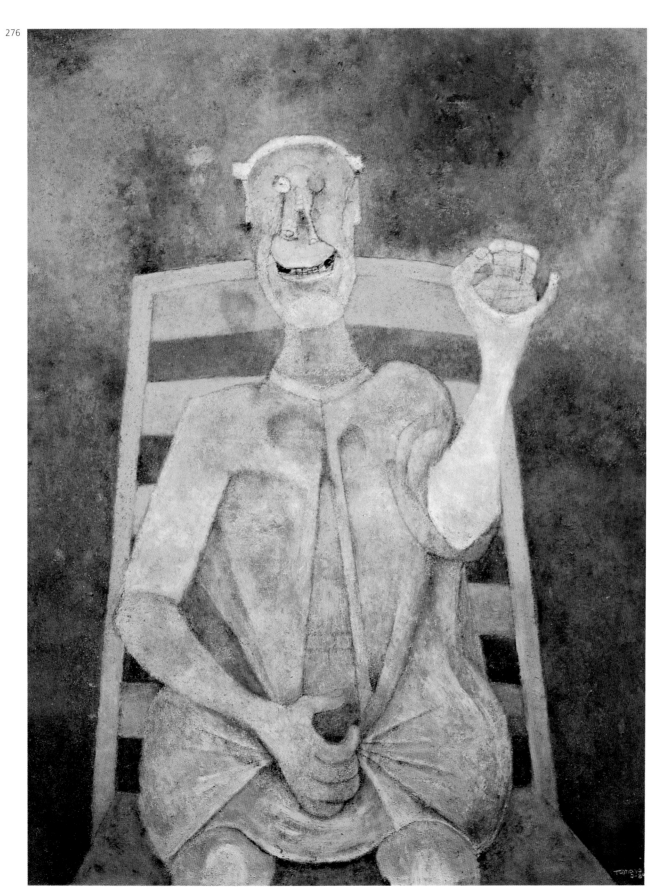

299

277

277
Character in an Interior (Personaje en un interior).
1989.
Oil on canvas, 37³/₈ × 51¹/₄ in. (95 × 130 cm).
Private collection, Mexico City.

278
Picasso Naked (Picasso al desnudo). 1989.
Oil on canvas, 51¹/₄ × 37⁵/₈ in. (130 × 95.5 cm).
Olga Tamayo Collection, Mexico City.

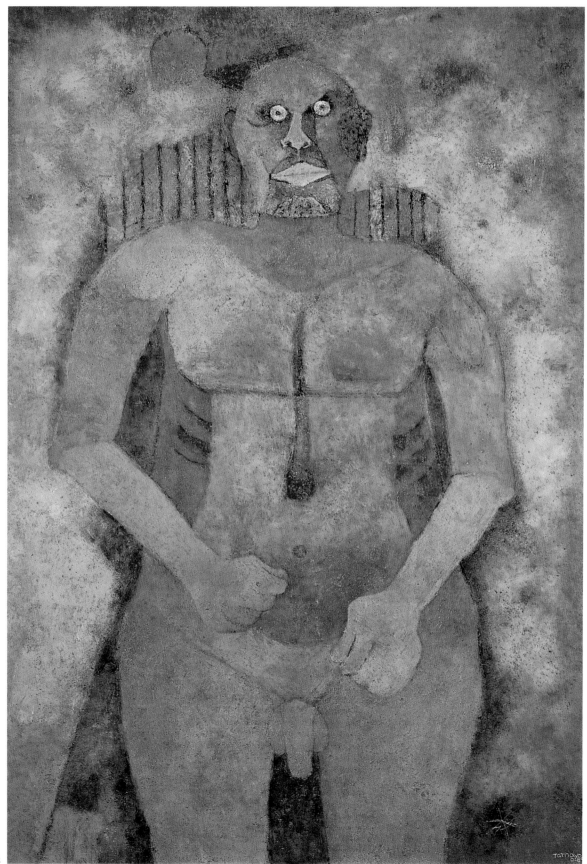

279
Man with a Flower
(Hombre con flor). 1989.
Oil on canvas, 33⁷/₈ × 26³/₈ in.
(86 × 67 cm).
Olga Tamayo Collection,
Mexico City.

280
The Vase with Flowers
(El vaso con flores). 1990.
Oil *on canvas*, 51¼ × 37³/₈ in.
(130 × 95 cm).
Marlborough Gallery,
New York, N.Y.

281
The Boy with the Bass Viol
(El muchacho del violón). 1990.
Oil on canvas, 51¼ × 37¾ in.
(130 × 96 cm).
Private collection Mexico City.

CHRONOLOGY

Rufino Tamayo, painter, muralist and lithographer, was born in Oaxaca, Mexico in 1899. In 1911 he moved to Mexico City and in 1917 he entered the Academy of Fine Arts there, which he left in 1921.
Tamayo lived in New York for twenty years and in Paris for twelve.

1921
Is appointed Chief of the Ethnographic Department (drawing) in the Museo Nacional de Arqueología, Mexico City.

1926
First one-man show in Mexico City. Visits New York for the first time and has his first one-man show in that city at the Weyhe Gallery.

1928-1929
Teaches painting at the Escuela Nacional de Bellas Artes, Mexico City.

1929
One-man show at the Teatro Nacional (now the Palacio de Bellas Artes), Mexico City.

1931
One-man show at the John Levy Galleries, New York.

1932
Is appointed chief of the Plastic Arts Department at the Secretaría de Educación Pública in Mexico City.

1933
Paints the mural *Music and Singing* for the Conservatorio Nacional de Música, Mexico City.

1934
Marries Olga Flores Rivas.

1935
One-man show at the Galería de Carolina Amor, Mexico City.

1936
Is appointed a member of the Mexican delegation to the Congress of Artists held in New York. Settles in that city for a long period. Teaches painting at the Dalton School.

1937
One-man shows at the Julien Levy Gallery in New York and the Howard Putzel Gallery in San Francisco.

1938
Paints the mural *Revolution* for the Museo Nacional de Antropología, Mexico City. One-man shows at the Galería de Arte Mexicano in Mexico City and the Catherine Kuh Gallery in Chicago.

1939
One-man show at the Valentine Gallery (Valentine Dudensing), New York.

1940
One-man show at the Valentine Gallery. Takes part in the exhibition "20 Centuries of Mexican Art" at the Museum of Modern Art, New York.

1942
One-man show at the Valentine Gallery, New York.

1943
Paints a mural for the Hillyer Art Library at Smith College, Northampton, Massachusetts.

1944
Exhibition at the Galería de Arte Mexicano, Mexico City.

1945
One-man show at the Arts Club, Chicago.

1946
Is appointed a teacher at the Brooklyn Museum (the Tamayo Studio). One-man show at the Valentine Gallery, New York.

1947
One-man shows at the Modern Art Society of the Cincinnati Art Museum, the Galería de Arte Mexicano in Mexico City, and the Valentine Gallery and Pierre Matisse Gallery in New York.

1948
Retrospective exhibition in homage to Tamayo on his completing twenty-five years as a painter held at the Palace of Arts, Mexico City.

1949
One-man show at the Galería de Arte Moderno Misrachi, Mexico City. Visits Europe and settles in Paris.

1950
Takes part in the Venice Biennale, at which three rooms are devoted to his work. One-man shows at the Galerie des Beaux-Arts in Paris, the Palais des Beaux-Arts in Brussels and the Knoedler Gallery, New York.

1951
One-man shows at the Instituto de Arte Moderno in Buenos Aires, the Salón de la Plástica Mexicana in Mexico City, the Frank Perls Gallery in Los Angeles and the Knoedler Gallery New York.

1952
Third prize at the Carnegie International Exhibition in Pittsburgh. Takes part in the exhibition "Art Mexicain du Précolumbien à nos jours" at the Musée National d'Art Moderne, Paris. Paints the murals *Birth of Our Nationality* and *Modern Mexico* for the Palacio de Bellas Artes, Mexico City. One-man shows at the Forth Worth Art Museum (Forth Worth, Texas) and the Panamerican Union, Washington, D.C.

1953
Grand Prix of Painting (together with Manessier) at the São Paulo Biennale in Brazil. Paints the mural *Man* for the Dallas Museum of Fine Arts, Dallas.

1954
One-man shows at the following galleries: Galería Excelsior and Salón de la Plástica Mexicana, Mexico City; Knoedler Gallery, New York; Frank Perls Gallery, Los Angeles; Santa Barbara Museum of Arts, Santa Barbara, California; San Francisco Museum of Arts, San Francisco, California.

1955
Second prize at the Carnegie International Exhibition, Pittsburgh. Paints the mural *América* for the Bank of the Southwest, Houston, Texas.

1956
One-man shows at the Galería Antonio Souza in Mexico City, the Museum of Fine Arts, Houston and the Knoedler Gallery, New York.

1957
Is made a Chevalier of the Legion d'Honneur by the French Government. Paints the mural *Prometheus* for the Library of the University of Puerto Rico.

1958
Paints a mural for the UNESCO building in Paris. Exhibition at the Galerie de France, Paris.

1959
Becomes a Corresponding Member of the Academia de Arte, Buenos Aires. One-man shows at the Kunsternes Hus in Oslo, the Felix Landau Gallery in Los Angeles and the Knoedler Gallery in New York. Takes part in "Documenta II" in Kassel, Germany.

1960
Awarded a prize by the Guggenheim International Foundation. One-man show at the Galerie de France, Paris. International Prize at the Bienal Interamericana de Mexico.

1961
Is elected a member of the Institute and Academy of Arts and Letters of the United States.

1962
One-man shows at the Galería Misrachi in Mexico and the Knoedler Gallery, New York.

1963
Paints the murals *Israel Yesterday* and *Israel Today* for the Israeli liner Shalom. Retrospective exhibition organized by the Mainichi newspaper chain in Tokyo. Travelling exhibition in Israel organized by the Israeli Museum Association.

1964
Is awarded the National Prize presented by the President of the Republic of Mexico, Adolfo López Mateos. Does 26 lithographs for the Ford Foundation (in editions of 20 each) at the Tamarind Workshop, Los Angeles. Paints the mural *Duality* for the Museo Nacional de Antropología, Mexico City.

1965
One-man show at the Galerie Semiha Huber, Zurich.

1966
Paints the mural *St Christopher* for the offices of Roberto García Mora, Mexico City.

1967
Paints the mural *The Mexican and His World* for the Mexican Pavilion at "Expo 67", Montreal.

1968
Retrospective exhibition to celebrate his fifty years as a painter, with 103 oils and lithographs, at the Palacio de Bellas Artes, Mexico City. Great exhibition of 124 works belonging to American collections at the Phoenix Art Museum, Phoenix, Arizona. Paints a mural for the Mexican Pavilion at the International Fair of San Antonio, Texas. One-man show at the National Museum of Art, Belgrade. Guest of honour with one-man exhibition at Venice Biennale.

1969
Does 20 lithographs at the Atelier Desjaubert in Paris for Touchstone and Co., New York. Paints the large mural *Energy* (75 square-metre) mural for the Club de Industriales de México at the Hotel Camino Real, Mexico City. Is awarded the Ibico Reggino Prize Reggio Calabria, sponsored by the President of Italy. Receives the Calouste Gulbenkian Prize, presented at the Institut de France, Paris.

1970
The French Government awards him the dignity of an Officiel de la Légion d'Honneur.

1971
Is made a Commendatore of the Italian Republic. One-man show at the Perls Gallery, New York. Paints the mural *Man Confronting Infinity* for the Hotel Camino Real in Mexico City, which is unveiled by the President of the Republic.

1972
The State of Oaxaca pays homage to Tamayo, naming him Favourite Son, awarding him the Juárez Medal and changing the name of one of the streets of its capital, Oaxaca de Juárez, from Calle de los Arcos to Calle de Rufino Tamayo.

1973
Does 15 lithographs for Ediciones Polígrafa of Barcelona and 5 lithographs for the publishing house of Giorgio Alessandrini in Rome. One-man shows at the Galería Misrachi in Mexico City and the Perls Gallery, New York.

1974
Donates a Museum of pre-Columbian Art, with 1,300 pieces, to the State of Oaxaca, his native land. Important ore-man show at the Musée d'Art Moderne de la Ville de Paris, with 100 oils painted in the sixties and seventies. The French Government names Tamayo a Knight Commander of the Order of Merit.

1975
Important exhibition (the same one as in Paris) at the Palazzo Strozzi, Florence. Is presented with the Medal of Florence at the Palazzo della Signoria and the Silver Plaque at the Palazzo dei Medici. Does 15 etchings for Ediciones Polígrafa, Barcelona.

1976
Exhibition at the Museo de Arte Moderno, Mexico City. One-man show at the Museum of Modern Art, Tokyo. Does 8 mixographs for Transworld Art of New York and 16 for Ediciones Polígrafa, Barcelona.

1977

Important exhibition to mark the opening of the Museo de Bellas Artes de Caracas, attended by the President of Venezuela, Carlos Andrés Pérez. Paints the mural *Total Eclipse* for the ALFA Industrial Company, Mexico City. Takes part in the 45th Biennale of São Paulo, at which he receives the homage of the entire continent with an exhibition consisting of 125 of his oils and 60 graphic works. Exhibition in his honour in San Salvador (El Salvador), where he is named an Honorary Citizen of the Republic. One-man show at the Marlborough Gallery, New York.

1978

One-man show at the Phillips Collection, Washington, D.C., under the auspices of the United States Government.

1979

Important exhibition at the Guggenheim Museum, New York, with 114 oils done between 1928 and 1979 and 3 murals. Another exhibition, of drawings, watercolours, gouaches and graphic work, at the Center for Inter-American Relations, New York. One-man show at the Marlborough Gallery, London. Does 15 etchings for Ediciones Polígrafa, Barcelona.

1981

Official opening, in May, of the Museo de Arte Contemporáneo Internacional Rufino Tamayo, in the Chapultepec Park, Mexico City. Tamayo donates to the people of Mexico his considerable collection of modern paintings, sculptures, drawings and tapestries by 174 artists from all over the world, as well as a superb collection of his own works. One-man show at the Marlborough Gallery, New York.

1982

Made Doctor Honoris Causa by the University of Southern California. One-man show at the Bernard Lewin Gallery, Beverly Hills, California. Produces the stained-glass piece *The Universe*. One-man show at the Marlborough Gallery, London.

1983

Exhibition "Rufino Tamayo: Graphik 1962-1982" at the Graphische Sammlung Albertina, Vienna. Produces the sculpture *The Conquest of Space* for San Francisco Airport. Awarded the Albert Einstein Prize by the Technion Society, Israel. One-man graphs show at the Museo Rufino Tamayo to present the monumental mixography *Two Characters Attacked by Dogs*.

1984

Made Foreign Correspondent Scholar by the St Luke Academy, Rome. One-man show in Tokyo organised by the Marlborough Gallery, New York.

1985

Retrospective exhibition of mixographies at the Bernard Lewin Gallery, Palm Springs, California. Contributes three lithographs to the portfolio dedicated to the Declaration of Human Rights. Among the other contributing artists are Tàpies, Chillida and Motherwell. Made member of the Royal Academy, London. King Juan Carlos of Spain awards him the Gold Medal of Merit in the Fine Arts. Is awarded one of the five prizes granted by the Frenchen Art Society, Switzerland, for his participation in the "10th International Triennial of Original Graphic Prints". Retrospective at the Museum of Modern Art, San Antonio, Texas.

1986

Retrospective of his work at the Museo de Monterrey. Homage is paid to him at the "VII Bienal de Grabado Interamericano y del Caribe" with a retrospective of his graphic work. The Museo Rufino Tamayo comes to form part of the circuit of museums of the Instituto Nacional de Bellas Artes. Retrospective at the Museo Regional de Guadalajara. Exhibition at the Bernard Lewin Gallery, Palm Springs, California.

1987

Retrospective at the Modern Museum of Art, Woodland Hills, California. Made Commandeur des Arts et des Lettres de France. Tamayo having completed seven decades of creative activity, the Mexican authorities decide to organice a National Homage at the Museo del Palacio de Bellas Artes and at the Museo Rufino Tamayo. The homage is also presented at cultural institutes and museums in the province of Mexico.

1988

Anthological exhibition at the Centro de Arte Reina Sofía, Madrid. Unveiling of his stained-glass *The Universe* in Monterrey in a specially designed and built pavilion. The Dominican government awards him the Orden de Cristóbal Colón. Awarded the Belisario Domínguez medal, the highest honour bestowed by the Mexican Government. Exhibition of graphic work at the Museo de Casas Reales, Santo Domingo.

1989

Awarded the Commendatore medal by the Italian government. Exhibition "Rufino Tamayo: Pintura y Gráfica" in the Main Hall of Plastic Artists, Moscow. The same show is subsequently presented in the Edvard Munch Museum, Oslo. Undergoes a delicate open-heart operation in Houston.

1990

The exhibition "Rufino Tamayo: Pintura y Gráfica" is inaugurated at the Ermitage Museum, Leningrad (today St Petersburg), later to be presented in the Staatliche Kunsthalle, Berlin. After a procese of restoration, the fresco mural *Music and Singing* is once again shown to the public in Mexico City. Exhibition of paintings from the eighties at the Marlborough Gallery, New York. Produces his last work: *The Boy with the Bass Viol*.

1991

In April the "Los Tamayo" old-people's home is opened in Oaxaca. On May 21 he is made member of El Colegio Nacional. On May 24 the government of the state of Veracruz pays homage to him by opening the Galería del Estado in Xalapa, with an exhibition of tris graphic work. Made Doctor Honoris Causa by the University of Veracruz. Rufino Tamayo dies in Mexico City on June 24. His body is mourned in the Palacio de Bellas Artes. His ashes are deposited in the Museo Rufino Tamayo.

MURALS

1933
Music and Singing. Fresco. Building of the former Conservatorio Nacional de Música (now the Prehistory Department of the Instituto Nacional de Antropología), Mexico City.

1937
Revolution. Fresco (fragment). Former Museo Nacional de Antropología (now the Museo de las Culturas), Mexico City.

1943
Nature and the Artist - The Work of Art and the Observer. Fresco. Hillyer Art Library, Smith College, Northampton, Massachusetts .

1952
Homage to the Indian Race. Vinyl on masonite. Instituto Nacional de Bellas Artes, Mexico City.

Birth of Our Nationality and *Mexico Today*. Vinyl on canvas. Museo Nacional de Bellas Artes, Mexico City.

Man. Vinyl on masonite. Dallas Museum of Fine Arts, Dallas, Texas.

1954
Day and Night. Vinyl on masonite. Sandborn's, Paseo de la Reforma, Mexico City.

Still Life. Vinyl on masonite. Sandborn's, Paseo de la Reforma, Mexico City.

1956
America. Vinyl on canvas. Private collection.

1957
Prometheus. Vinyl on canvas. Library of the University of Puerto Rico Río Piedras, Puerto Rico.

1958
Prometheus Bringing Fire to Man. Vinyl on canvas. Lecture Hall, UNESCO, Paris.

1963
Israel Yesterday - Israel Today. Vinyl on canvas. The liner Shalom of the Israel Ocean Liner Company, now Private collection.

1964
Duality. Vinyl on canvas. Museo Nacional de Antropología, Mexico City.

1966
St Christopher. Vinyl on canvas. Private office of Sr. Roberto García Mora, Mexico City.

1967
The Mexican and His World. Vinyl on canvas. Mexican Pavilion at "Expo 67", Montreal. Later installed in the Ministerio de Relaciones Exteriores, Mexico City.

1968
Brotherhood. Vinyl on canvas. Mexican Pavilion at the International Fair of San Antonio, Texas. Later installed in the Ministerio de Relaciones Exteriores, Mexico City.

1969
Fire. Vinyl on canvas. Club de Industriales de México. Hotel Camino Real, Mexico City.

1970
Man Confronting Infinity. Vinyl on canvas. Hotel Camino Real . Mexico City.

1977
Total Eclipse. Vinyl on canvas. Sociedad Industrial ALFA, Mexico City.

MONUMENTAL SCULPTURES AND WORKS

1980
Homage to the Sun. Iron sculpture 27 metres high, for the Mayor's Office, Monterrey, Nuevo León, Mexico. Donated by the artist.

1982
The Universe. Stained glass, 8×6.8 m. Six years later installed in a pavilion of the Centro Cultural Alfa, Monterrey, Nuevo León.

1983
The Conquest of Space. Sculpture steel. San Francisco Airport, California.

BASIC BIBLIOGRAPHY

ALANIS, Judith and Sofía URRUTIA. *Rufino Tamayo, una cronología. 1899-1987.* INBA/SEP. Museo Rufino Tamayo, Mexico City, 1987.

ALBA, Víctor. *Coloquios de Coyoacán con Rufino Tamayo.* B. Costa-Amic Editor, Colección Panoramas, No. 4, Mexico City, 1950.

CARDOZA Y ARAGÓN, Luis. *Rufino Tamayo.* Galería de artistas mexicanos contemporáneos, publicaciones del Palacio de Bellas Artes, Mexico City, 1934.

—*Pintura mexicana contemporánea.* UNAM, Mexico City, 1953.

FERNÁNDEZ, Justino. *Rufino Tamayo.* Instituto de Investigaciones Estéticas, UNAM, Mexico City, 1948.

—*Arte moderno contemporáneo de México.* Instituto de Investigaciones Estéticas, UNAM, Mexico City, 1952.

GARCÍA PONCE, Juan. *Tamayo.* Galería de Arte Misrachi, Mexico City, 1967.

GENAUER, Emily (Pulitzer Price). *Tamayo.* Harry N. Abrams, Inc., New York, 1974.

GOLDWATER, Robert. *Tamayo.* The Quadrangle Press, New York, 1947.

GUAL, Enrique. *Rufino Tamayo.* Eugenio Fishgrund editor, Mexico City.

—*Drawings by Tamayo.* Ediciones Mexicanas, S.A., Mexico City, 1950.

MANRIQUE, Jorge Alberto. *"Introducción al arte contemporáneo en México".* Historia del Arte Mexicano, No. 91. SEP/INBA. Salvat, Mexico City, 1982.

PALENCIA, Ceferino. *Rufino Tamayo.* Ediciones de Arte. Colección Anáhuac de Arte Mexicano, No. 24, Mexico City, 1950.

—*Arte contemporáneo en Mexico.* Colección Cultura para Todos. Editorial Porrúa, Mexico City, 1951.

PAZ, Octavio. *Tamayo en la pintura mexicana.* UNAM. Colección de Ate, No. 6, Mexico City, 1959.

PAZ, Octavio and Jacques LASSAIGNE. *Rufino Tamayo.* Ediciones Polígrafa, Barcelona, 1982.

Rufino Tamayo: Myth and Magic. The Solomon R. Guggenheim Foundation, New York, 1979.

TIBOL, Raquel. *Orozco, Rivera, Siqueiros, Tamayo.* Colección Testimonios. Fondo de Cultura Económica, Mexico City, 1974.

TIBOL, Raquel (Coord.) *et. al. Rufino Tamayo. 70 años de creación.* INBA/SEP. Museo Rufino Tamayo, Mexico City, 1987.

—(Comp.) *Textos de Rufino Tamayo.* UNAM, Mexico City, 1987.

—(Selec.) *Rufino Tamayo, una antología crítica.* CREA/Terra Nova. Colección Grandes Maestros Mexicanos, No. 13, Mexico City, 1987.

WESTHEIM, Paul. *El Arte de Tamayo una investigación estética.* Artes de Mexico City, 1956.

FILMS

Cómo nace un Mural. Universidad Nacional de Mexico City, 1965.

Rufino Tamayo. B.B.C. Films, London, 1966.

Tamayo. Directed by Max Pol Fouchet, Paris, 1970.

The Artistic Life of Rufino Tamayo. Produced and directed by Gary Conklin, Los Angeles, 1973.

LIST OF WORKS

1
Boy in Blue (Niño en azul). 1928.
Oil on canvas, 29½ × 25⅛ in. (75 × 63.8 cm).
Olga Tamayo Collection, Mexico City.

2
Arrangement of objects (Arreglo de objetos).
1928.
Oil on canvas, 19¾ × 25⅝ in. (50 × 65 cm).
Bernard Lewin Collection, Los Angeles, California.

3
Still life (Naturaleza muerta). 1928.
Oil on canvas, 22½ × 18¾ in. (57 × 47.5 cm).
Bernard Lewin Collection, Los Angeles, California.

4
Shells (Los caracoles). 1929.
Oil on canvas, 23¾ × 24¾ in. (59 × 63 cm).
Olga Tamayo Collection, Mexico City.

5
Yellow Chair (Silla amarilla). 1929.
Oil on canvas, 28¾ × 25 in. (73 × 63.5 cm).
Olga Tamayo Collection, Mexico City.

6
Mandolines and Pineapples (Mandolinas y piñas).
1930.
Oil on canvas, 19¾ × 27⅝ in. (50.2 × 70 cm).
The Phillips Collection, Washington, D.C.

7
Nude in Grey (Desnudo en gris). 1931.
Oil on canvas, 35 × 25¼ in. (89 × 64 cm).
Museo de Arte Moderno/I.N.B.A., Mexico City.

8
Homage to Juárez (Homenaje a Juárez). 1932.
Oil on canvas, 23⅝ × 29½ in. (60 × 75 cm).
Museo de Arte Moderno/I.N.B.A., Mexico City.

9
Homage to Zapata (Homenaje a Zapata). 1935.
Oil on canvas, 25⅝ × 21¾ in. (65 × 54 cm).
Mr and Mrs Herman Weitz Collection, Mexico City.

10
Photogenic Venus (Venus fotogénica). 1934.
Oil on canvas, 29½ × 39⅜ in. (75 × 100 cm).
Secretaría de Hacienda y Crédito Público,
Mexico City.

11
The Musicians (Los músicos). 1934.
Oil on canvas, 31½ × 39⅜ in. (80 × 100 cm).
Cummins Catherwood Collection,
Saratoga Springs, N.Y.

12
Still Life (Naturaleza muerta). 1937.
Oil on canvas, 39⅜ × 53⅛ in. (100 × 135 cm).
Robert Brady Foundation, Cuernavaca, Mexico.

13
Fruit Vendors (Vendedoras de fruta). 1938.
Oil on canvas, 17¼ × 23¾ in. (43.8 × 60.3 cm).
Zuinaga Aguilar de García Collection Mexico City.

14
Women of Tehuantepec (Mujeres de Tehuantepec).
1939.
Oil on canvas, 34¼ × 57⅛ in. (87 × 145 cm).
Albright-Knox Art Gallery, Buffalo, N.Y.

15
*Woman with Birdcage (Mujer con jaula de
pájaros)*. 1941.
Oil on canvas, 41½ × 32½ in. (105.4 × 82.5 cm).
The Art Institute of Chicago, Illinois.

16
Carnival (Carnaval). 1941.
Oil on canvas, 43¼ × 33⅛ in. (110 × 84 cm).
The Phillips Collection, Washington, D.C.

17
Woman with Pineapple (Mujer con piña). 1941.
Oil on canvas, 40 × 30 in. (101.6 × 76.2 cm).
The Museum of Modern Art, New York.

18
Two Dogs (Dos perros). 1941.
Oil on canvas, 31½ × 40¼ in. (76.9 × 102.3 cm).
Museum of Modern Art, Houston, Texas.

19
Lion and Horse (León y caballo). 1942.
Oil on canvas, 36 × 46 in. (91.5 × 116.8 cm).
Washington University Gallery of Art, St. Louis
Missouri.

20
Animals (Animales). 1941.
Oil on canvas, 30⅜ × 39⅜ in. (77 × 100 cm).
The Museum of Modern Art, New York.

21
Woman Calling (Mujer llamando). 1941.
Oil on canvas, 36 × 24 in. (91.5 × 61 cm).
Lee A. Ault Collection, New York.

22
*Two Galloping Horses in Red and Brown
(Dos caballos corriendo, en rojo y café)*. 1942.
Oil on canvas, 34 × 46¾ in. (86.2 × 118.8 cm).
Private collection, Monterrey.

23
Woman Spinning (Mujer hilando). 1943.
Oil on canvas, 42 × 33 in. (106.7 × 83.9 cm).
Roy R. Newberger Collection.

24
*Nature and the Artist - The Work of Art and the
Observer (La naturaleza y el artista - La obra de
arte y el espectador)*. 1943.

Fresco, at present transferred by means of
strappo technic to 22 moving panels,
9 ft. 8½ in. × 43 ft. 6⅞ in. (2.95 × 13.28 m).
Hillyer Library, Smith College Massachusetts.
Commissioned to the artist by Jere Abbot in
honourof Mrs Elizabeth Cutter Morrow.

25
The Flute-Player (El flautista). 1944.
Oil on canvas 45 × 37¼ in. (114.4 × 94.5 cm).
IBM Corporation, Armonk, N.Y.

26
Bird Charmer (Encantador de pájaros). 1945.
Oil on canvas, 61 × 50¾ in. (155 × 129 cm).
Private collection, New York.

27
*Woman Dressing Her Hair (Mujer arreglándose el
pelo)*. 1944.
Gouache, 29 × 22⅞ in. (73.5 × 58 cm).
Private collection, U.S.A.

28
Woman and Bird (Mujer y pájaro). 1944.
Oil on canvas, 42 × 34 in. (106.7 × 86.3 cm).
The Cleveland Museum of Art. Leonard C. Hanna
Jr. Collection, Cleveland, Ohio.

29
Portrait of Olga (Retrato de Olga). 1945.
Oil on canvas, 48 × 35 in. (122 × 89 cm).
Mr and Mrs Ralph F. Colin Collection, New York.

30
*Women Reaching for the Moon (Mujeres
alcanzando la luna)*. 1946.
Oil on canvas, 36¼ × 26 in. (92 × 66 cm).
The Cleveland Museum of Art. Donated by the
Leonard C. Hanna Fund, Cleveland, Ohio.

31
Dancers Over the Sea (Danzantes frente al mar).
1945.
Oil on canvas, 30 × 40 in. (76.2 × 101.6 cm).
Cincinnati Art Museum. Donated by Mr Lee Ault,
Cincinnati, Ohio.

32
Total Eclipse (Eclipse total). 1946.
Oil on canvas, 40 × 30 in. (101.6 × 76.2 cm).
Fogg Art Museum, Harvard University,
Cambridge, Massachusetts.

33
The Shout (El grito). 1947.
Oil on canvas, 40 × 30 in. (101.6 × 76.2 cm).
Galleria Nazionale d'Arte Moderna, Rome.

34
Lollipop (Piruli). 1949.
Oil on canvas, 38⅝ × 31½ in. (98 × 80 cm).
Mr and Mrs Stephen Simon Collection, New York.

35
Man Before the Infinite (El hombre ante el infinito). 1950.
Oil on canvas, 37³/₈×53¹/₈ in. (95×135 cm).
Musées Royaux des Beaux-Arts, Brussels.

36
Man with Guitar (Hombre con guitarra). 1950.
Oil on canvas, 76³/₄×51¹/₄ in. (195×130 cm).
Musée National d'Art Moderne, Centre d'Art et de Culture Georges Pompidou, Paris.

37
The Tormented (El atormentado). 1949
Oil on canvas, 39³/₈×31¹/₂ in. (100×80 cm).
Private collection, Japan.

38
Man with Cigar (Hombre con puro). 1950.
Oil on canvas, 32¹/₈×25³/₄ in. (81.5×65.5 cm).
Mr and Mrs Stephen Simon Collection, New York.

39
Nude in White (Desnudo en blanco). 1950.
Oil on canvas, 76³/₈×50³/₄ in. (194×129 cm).
Mr and Mrs Harry Pollack Collection, Longboat Key, Florida.

40
Cow Swatting Flies (Vaca espantándose las moscas). 1951.
Oil on canvas, 31¹/₈×39 in. (79×99 cm).
Humanities Research Center, The University of Texas, Austin, Texas.

41
Homage to the Indian Race (Homenaje a la raza india). 1952.
Vinelita on celotex 196⁷/₈×157¹/₂ in. (500×400 cm).
Museo Rufino Tamayo/I.N.B.A., Mexico City.

42
Sunset (Anochecer). 1953.
Oil on masonite, 11³/₄×31¹/₂ in. (29.8×80 cm).
Private Collection.

43
Supersonic Plane (Avión más rápido que el sonido). 1954.
Oil on canvas, 21¹/₄×29¹/₂ in. (54×75 cm).
Dr Jaime Constantiner Collection, Mexico.

44
The Burning Man (El quemado). 1955.
Oil on canvas, 39³/₈×31¹/₂ in. (100×80 cm).
Rogerio and Lorenza Azcárraga Collection, Mexico City.

45
Cosmic Terror (Terror cósmico). 1954.
Oil on canvas, 41³/₄×30 in. (106×76 cm).
Museo de Arte Moderno/I.N.B.A., Mexico City.

46
Telephonitis (Telefonitis). 1957.
Oil in canvas, 39³/₈×32 in. (100×81.3 cm).
Nasjonalgalleriet, Oslo.

47
White Watermelons (Sandías en blanco). 1956.
Oil on canvas, 31¹/₂×39³/₈ in. (80×100 cm).
Olga Azcárraga Collection, Mexico City.

48
Night of Mysteries (Noche de misterios). 1957.
Oil on canvas, 39³/₈×32 in. (100×81.3 cm).
Nasjonalgalleriet, Oslo.

49
Insomnia (Insomnio). 1958.
Oil on canvas, 38¹/₂×57¹/₈ in. (97.8×145 cm).
Francisco Osio Morales Collection, Mexico City.

50
Prometheus Bringing Fire to Mankind (Prometeo entregando el fuego a los hombres). 1958.
Fresco 196⁷/₈×177 in. (500×450 cm).
Lecture Hall, UNESCO, Paris.

51
Woman in White (Mujer en blanco). 1959.
Oil on canvas, 76³/₄×51¹/₄ in. (195×130 cm).
Milwaukee Art Center. Donated by Mr and Mrs Harry L. Bradley, Milwaukee, Wisconsin.

52
Woman in Grey (Mujer en gris). 1959.
Oil on canvas, 76³/₄×51¹/₄ in. (195×130 cm).
The Solomon R. Guggenheim Museum, New York.

53
Children Playing (Niños jugando). 1959.
Oil on canvas, 51¹/₄×76³/₄ in. (130.2×195 cm).
Mr and Mrs Ralph F. Collin Collection, New York.

54
Man with a Guitar (Hombre con una guitarra). 1959.
Oil on canvas, 37³/₈×53¹/₈ in. (95×135 cm).
Private collection, U.S.A.

55
Children's Game (Juego de niños). 1960.
Oil on canvas, 53¹/₈×76³/₄ in. (135×195 cm).
Rafaela Arocena de Ussía Collection, Paris.

56
Man with Flower (Hombre con flor). 1960.
Oil on canvas, 50¹/₂×38 in. (128.3×96.5 cm).
Hannelore B. Chulhof Collection, New York.

57
Composition (Composición). 1960.
Oil on canvas, 37³/₈×53¹/₈ in. (95×135 cm).
Musée National d'Art Moderne, Centre d'Art et de Culture Georges Pompidou, Paris.

58
The Coffeepot (La cafetera). 1960.
Oil on canvas, 53¹/₈×76³/₄ in. (135×195 cm).
Bernard Lewin Collection, Los Angeles, California.

59
Women (Mujeres). 1960.
Oil on canvas, 54×76³/₄ in. (137×195 cm).
Arnold and Elaine Horwitch Collection, Phoenix, Arizona.

60
Two Characters (Dos personajes). 1961.
Oil on canvas, 37³/₈×51¹/₄ in. (95×130 cm).
Mimi Indaco Collection, Mexico.

61
Woman in Front of a Looking-Glass (Mujer frente al espejo). 1960.
Oil on canvas, 39³/₈×31¹/₂ in. (100×80 cm).
Private collection, Mexico.

62
Couple (Pareja). 1960.
Oil on canvas, 50³/₄×77 in. (129×195.5 cm).
Bernard Lewin Collection, Los Angeles, California.

63
Two Figures in Blue (Dos figuras en azul). 1961.
Oil on canvas, 31⁷/₈×39³/₈ in. (81×100 cm).
Museo de Bellas Artes, Caracas.

64
Couple in Red (Pareja en rojo). 1961.
Oil on canvas, 38⁵/₈×51⁵/₈ in. (98×131 cm).
Jorge Díaz Serrano Collection, Mexico City.

65
Mountainous Landscape (Paisaje serrano). 1961.
Oil on canvas, 53¹/₈×76³/₄ in. (135×195 cm).
Museo de Arte Moderno/I.N.B.A., Mexico City.

66
Meeting (Encuentro). 1961.
Oil on canvas, 53¹/₈×76³/₄ in. (135×195 cm).
Museo de Arte Moderno/I.N.B.A., Mexico City.

67
Figure (Figura). 1961.
Oil on canvas, 17³/₄×21⁵/₈ in. (45×55 cm).
Bernard Lewin Collection, Los Angeles, California

68
Head with Blue Hat (Cabeza con sombrero azul). 1962.
Oil on canvas, 15³/₄×19³/₄ in. (40×50 cm).
Bernard Lewin Collection, Los Angeles, California

69
Woman in Front of a Looking-Glass (Mujer ante el espejo). 1961.
Oil on canvas, 39³/₈×31¹/₂ in. (100×80 cm).
Private collection, Mexico City.

70
Winding Road (Camino sinuoso). 1962.
Oil on canvas, 31⁷/₈ × 39³/₈ in. (81 × 100 cm).
Pivate collection, Mexico City.

71
Afternoon Sun (Sol de tarde). 1962.
Oil on canvas, 31¹/₂ × 39³/₈ in. (80 × 100 cm).
Neda Anhalt Collection, Mexico City.

72
Man's Profile (Perfil de hombre). 1962.
Oil on canvas, 31¹/₂ × 39³/₈ in. (80 × 100 cm).
Private collection, Mexico.

73
Two figures (Dos figuras). 1962.
Oil on canvas, 39³/₈ × 29¹/₂ in. (100 × 75 cm).
Private collection, Mexico City.

74
Three Characters and a Bird (Tres personajes y un pajero). 1962.
Oil on canvas, 53¹/₈ × 76³/₄ in. (135 × 195 cm).
Museo de Arte Moderno/l.N.B.A., Mexico City.

75
Taurus (Tauro). 1962.
Oil on canvas, 38¹/₄ × 51¹/₄ in. (97 × 130 cm).
Bernard Lewin Collection, Los Angeles, California.

76
Man with Red Hat (Hombre con sombrero rojo). 1963.
Oil on canvas, 51⁵/₈ × 38¹/₄ in. (131 × 97.2 cm).
Museo de Arte Moderno/l.N.B.A., Mexico City.

77
Two Characters (Dos personajes). 1967.
Oil on canvas, 39³/₈ × 31¹/₂ in. (100 × 80 cm).
Dorsky Gallery, New York.

78
Boy at the Window (Muchacho en la ventana). 1963.
Oil on canvas, 18⁷/₈ × 25⁵/₈ in. (48 × 65 cm).
Bernard Lewin Collection, Los Angeles, California.

79
Man (Hombre). 1961.
Oil on canvas, 29¹/₂ × 36⁵/₈ in. (75 × 93 cm).
Knoedler Gallery, New York.

80
Black Venus (Venus negra). 1965.
Oil on canvas, 39³/₈ × 32 in. (100 × 81.2 cm).
Private collection, Mexico City.

81
Couple (Pareja). 1965.
Oil on canvas, 39³/₈ × 31¹/₂ in. (100 × 80 cm).
Eli Klein Collection, Mexico.

82
The Smoker (El fumador). 1965.
Oil on canvas, 31¹/₂ × 26³/₈ in. (80 × 67 cm).
Angel Céspedes Collection, Mexico.

83
Portrait of Olga (Retrato de Olga). 1964.
Oil on canvas, 82⁵/₈ × 53¹/₈ in. (210 × 135 cm).
Museo Rufino Tamayo/l.N.B.A., Mexico City.

84
Family (Familia). 1965.
Oil on canvas, 31¹/₂ × 39³/₈ in. (80 × 100 cm).
Licio Lagos Collection, Mexico.

85
Portrait of Boys (Retrato de muchachos). 1966.
Oil on canvas, 37⁷/₈ × 53¹/₈ in. (95 × 135 cm).
Mayalen Zunzunegui Collection, Mexico.

86
The Juggler (El juglar). 1966.
Oil on canvas, 31¹/₂ × 39³/₈ in. (80 × 100 cm).
Ana Misrachi Collection, Mexico.

87
Couple in the Garden (Pareja en el jardín). 1966.
Oil on canvas, 53¹/₈ × 76³/₄ in. (135 × 195 cm).
Fernando Casas Bernard Collection, Mexico City.

88
Dancers (Danzantes). 1966.
Oil on canvas 51¹/₄ × 76³/₄ in. (130 × 195 cm).
Mr and Mrs Leon Davidoff Collection, Mexico City.

89
Three Women (Tres mujeres). 1966.
Oil on canvas, 38¹/₄ × 51¹/₄ in. (97 × 130 cm).
Jaime Constantiner Collection, Mexico.

90
The Man with the Stick (Hombre del bastón). 1966.
Oil on canvas, 38³/₄ × 31¹/₂ in. (98.5 × 80 cm).
René Becerra Collection, Mexico City.

91
Women in Repose (Mujeres en reposo). 1966.
Oil on canvas, 53¹/₈ × 76³/₄ in. (135 × 195 cm).
Carlos Hank Rohn Collection, Mexico.

92
Self-Portrait (Autorretrato). 1967.
Oil on canvas, 68⁷/₈ × 49¹/₄ in. (175 × 125 cm).
Museo de Arte Moderno/l.N.B.A., Mexico City.

93
Three Women in Profile (Tres mujeres de perfil). 1967.
Oil on canvas, 51¹/₄ × 76³/₄ in. (130 × 195 cm).
Lina Klein Collection, Mexico.

94
Carnival (Carnaval). 1967.
Oil on canvas 53¹/₈ × 37³/₈ in.(135 × 95 cm).
Private collection, Monterrey.

95
The Mexican and His World (El mexicano y su mundo). 1967.
Mural, 196⁷/₈ × 53¹/₈ in. (500 × 135 cm).
Secretaría de Relaciones Exteriores, Mexico City.

96
The Mexican and His World (El mexicano y su mundo) (detall). 1967.
Mural, 196⁷/₈ × 53¹/₈ in. (500 × 135 cm).
Secretaría de Relaciones Exteriores, Mexico City.

97
Three Figures (Tres figuras). 1966.
Oil on canvas, 51¹/₄ × 76³/₄ in. (130 × 195 cm).
Moisés Tanur Collection, Mexico City.

98
Three Figures in Red (Tres figuras en rojo). 1967.
Oil on canvas, 53¹/₈ × 76³/₄ in. (135 × 195 cm).
José Guindi Collection, Mexico.

99
Man with Big Hat (Hombre con gran sombrero). 1967.
Oil on canvas, 31¹/₂ × 39³/₈ in. (80 × 100 cm).
Private Collection, Miami, Florida.

100
Marriage Portrait (Retrato matrimonial). 1967.
Oil on canvas, 53¹/₂ × 76³/₄ in. (136 × 195 cm).
Bernard Lewin Collection, Los Angeles, California.

101
Total Eclipse (Eclipse total). 1967.
Oil on canvas, 13 × 21⁵/₈ in. (33 × 55 cm).
Rodney Madeiros Collection, San Francisco.

102
Three Characters in Red (Tres personajes en rojo). 1970.
Oil on canvas 51¹/₄ × 76³/₄ in. (130 × 195 cm).
Jacobo Zabludowsky Collection Mexico City.

103
Man Glowing with Happiness (Hombre radiante de alegría). 1968.
Oil on canvas 37³/₈ × 51¹/₄ in. (95 × 130 cm).
Museo de Arte Moderno/l.N.B.A., Mexico City.

104
The Man with the Bells (El hombre de los cascabeles). 1965.
Oil on canvas, 39³/₈ × 31¹/₂ in. (100 × 80 cm).
Bernard Lewin Collection, Los Angeles, California.

105
Character (Personaje). 1968.
Oil on canvas, 31¹/₂ × 39³/₈ in. (80 × 100 cm).
Bernard Lewin Collection, Los Angeles, California.

106
Pelota Players (Jugadores de pelota). 1968.
Oil on canvas, 37³/₈×51¼ in. (95×130 cm).
Moisés Tanur Collection Mexico City.

107
Watermelons (Sandías). 1968.
Oil on canvas, 51¼×76³/₄ in. (130×195 cm).
Museo Rufino Tamayo/I.N.B.A., Mexico City.

108
Torsos (Torsos). 1968.
Oil on canvas, 31½×39³/₈ in. (80×100 cm).
Museo de Arte Moderno/I.N.B.A., Mexico City.

109
A Man and a Woman (Un hombre y una mujer).
1969.
Oil on canvas, 39³/₈×31½ in. (100×80 cm).
Abraham Zabludowsky Collection Mexico City.

110
Man Sticking Out His Tongue (Hombre sacando la lengua). 1967.
Oil on canvas, 39³/₈×31⁷/₈ in. (100×81 cm).
Moisés Tanur Collection, Mexico City.

111
Head (Cabeza). 1968.
Oil on canvas, 23⁵/₈×15³/₄ in. (60×40 cm).
Orme Lewis Collection Scotland.

112
Showcase (Aparador). 1968.
Oil on canvas, 53¹/₈×37³/₈ in. (135×95 cm).
Bernard Lewin Collection, Los Angeles, California.

113
Character in Reds and Yellows (Personaje en rojos y amarillos). 1969.
Oil on canvas, 39³/₈×31½ in. (100×80 cm).
Luis Arzae Collection , Mexico City.

114
Two Children Playing (Dos niños jugando). 1967.
Oil on canvas, 53¹/₈×76³/₄ in. (135×195 cm).
Private collection, Mexico City.

115
Two Figures and the Moon (Dos figuras y la luna).
1970.
Oil on canvas, 31½×39³/₈ in. (80×100 cm*)*.
Private collection.

116
Torso of a Man (Torso de hombre). 1969.
Oil on canvas, 39³/₈×31½ in. (100×80 cm).
Emily Genauer Collection, New York.

117
Man in Black (Hombre en negro). 1969.
Oil on canvas, 39³/₈×31½ in. (100×80 cm).
Private collection, Mexico.

118
Head (Cabeza). 1969.
Oil on canvas, 39³/₈×33½ in. (100×85 cm).
Weinberg Collection, Chicago, Illinois.

119
Man and Woman (Hombre y mujer). 1970.
Oil on canvas, 53¹/₈×37³/₈ in. (135×95 cm).
Peter G. Wray Collection, Phoenix, Arizona.

120
Man in Grey (Hombre en gris). 1970.
Oil on canvas, 39³/₈×31½ in. (100×80 cm).
Manuel Espinosa Iglesias Collection, Mexico City.

121
Figure on a White Background (Figura sobre un fondo blanco). 1970.
Oil on canvas, 39³/₈×31¹/₈ in. (100×79 cm).
William Link and Margery Nelson Collection,
Los Angeles, California.

122
Man's torso (Torso de hombre). 1970.
Oil on canvas, 39³/₈×31½ in. (100×80 cm).
Bernard Lewin Collection, Los Angeles, California.

123
Floating Sphere (Esfera flotante). 1970.
Oil on canvas, 13³/₄×19³/₄ in. (35×50 cm).
Harry Weinstock Collection, New York.

124
Two Figures and the Moon (Dos figuras y la luna). 1970.
Oil on canvas, 39³/₈×31½ in. (100×80 cm).
Manuel Ulloa Collection, Madrid.

125
Figures (Figuras). 1970.
Oil on canvas, 76³/₄×53¹/₈ in. (195×135 cm).
Luigi Bolla Collection, Milan.

126
The Loner (El solitario). 1970.
Oil on canvas, 53¹/₈×37³/₈ in. (135×95 cm).
Mortimer C. Lebowitz Collection, Maclean, Virginia.

127
Woman in Front of a Looking-Glass (Mujer delante del espejo). 1970.
Oil on canvas 51¼×37³/₈ in.(130×95 cm).
Museo de Arte Moderno/I.N.B.A., Mexico City.

128
Character in an Interior (Personaje en un interior). 1970.
Oil on canvas, 51¼×37³/₈ in. (130×95 cm).
Jacobo Zabludowsky Collection, Mexico City.

129
Character in Black (Personaje en negro). 1970.
Oil on canvas 33½×43¹/₈ in. (85×110 cm).
Alexander Calder Collection, Saché, France.

130
Two Characters in an Interior (Dos personajes en un interior). 1970.
Oil on canvas, 38¼×51¼ in. (97×130 cm).
Leo Bakalar Collection, Boston, Massachusetts.

131
Three Characters (Tres personajes). 1970.
Oil on canvas, 39³/₈×52 in. (100×132 cm).
Stewen Jacobsen Collection, New York.

132
Head in Red (Cabeza en rojo). 1970.
Oil on canvas, 13³/₄×19³/₄ in. (35×50 cm).
Caroline Marcuse Collection, New York.

133
Two Figures in Yellow (Dos figuras en amarillo).
1971.
Oil on canvas, 11⁷/₈×15³/₄ in. (30×40 cm).
Irving Richards Collection, New York.

134
Man in Red (Hombre en rojo). 1970.
Oil on canvas, 76³/₄×53¹/₈ in. (195×135 cm).
Mauricio Menache Collection, Mexico.

135
Two Women in Space (Dos mujeres en el espacio). 1970.
Oil on canvas, 51¼×38¼ in. (130×97 cm).
Sidney Berkowitz Collection, Philadelphia.

136
Slanting Figure and Its Shadow (Figura inclinada y su sombra). 1971.
Oil on canvas, 33½×43¼ in. (85×110 cm).
Private Collection, Mexico.

137
Man in Yellow (Hombre en amarillo). 1970.
Oil on canvas, 17³/₄×13³/₄ in. (45×35 cm).
Isaac Besudo Collection, Mexico.

138
Man and His Shadow (Hombre y su sombra). 1971
Oil on canvas, 19³/₄×15³/₄ in. (50×40 cm).
Museo de Arte Moderno/I.N.B.A., Mexico City.

139
Encounter (Reencuentro). 1972.
Oil on canvas, 53³/₈×37³/₈ in. (135×95 cm).
Fuji International Co. Collection, Tokyo.

140
Family Playing (Familia jugando). 1971.
Oil on canvas, 51¼×76³/₄ in. (130×195 cm).
Latin American Masters Collection, Los Angeles,
California.

141
Women (Mujeres). 1971.
Oil on canvas, 53¹/₈×76³/₄ in. (135×195 cm).
Museo Rufino Tamayo/I.N.B.A., Mexico City.

142
Character (Personaje).
Oil on canvas, 13³/₄ × 7⁷/₈ in. (35 × 20 cm).
Peter G. Wray Collection Phoenix Arizona.

143
Figure in Motion (Figura en movimiento). 1971.
Oil on canvas, 15³/₄ × 9⁷/₈ in. (40 × 25 cm).
Michel Barr Collection, New York.

144
Head (Cabeza). 1971.
Oil on canvas, 13³/₄ × 7⁷/₈ in. (35 × 20 cm).
Private collection, U.S.A.

145
Man and Woman (Hombre y mujer). 1971.
Oil on canvas 31¹/₂ × 27⁵/₈ in. (80 × 70 cm).
Norton Walbridge Collection, La Jolla.

146
Character (Personaje). 1972.
Oil on canvas, 39³/₈ × 31⁷/₈ in. (100 × 81 cm).
Víctor Bravo Ahuja Collection, Mexico City.

147
Figure in Red and Black (Figura en rojo y negro).
1971.
Oil on canvas, 17³/₄ × 25⁵/₈ in. (45 × 65 cm).
Winifred Breuning Collection, Oaxaca, Mexico.

148
Hippy. 1972.
Oil on canvas, 51¹/₄ × 37³/₈ in. (130 × 95 cm).
Museo de Arte Moderno/I.N.B.A., Mexico City.

149
Portrait of Dubuffet (Retrato de Dubuffet). 1972.
Oil on canvas, 31¹/₂ × 39³/₈ in. (80 × 100 cm).
Museo de Arte Moderno/I.N.B.A., Mexico City.

150
Head in Green (Cabeza en verde). 1972.
Oil on canvas, 39³/₈ × 31¹/₂ in. (100 × 80 cm).
Bernard Lewin Collection, Los Angeles, California.

151
Man's Head (Cabeza de hombre). 1972.
Oil on canvas 39³/₈ × 31¹/₂ in.(100 × 80 cm).
J. H. Sherman Collection Baltimore Maryland.

152
Eroded Landscape (Tierra erosionada). 1972.
Oil on canvas 37³/₈ × 51¹/₄ in. (95 × 130 cm).
Armando Garza Sada Coilection, Monterrey.

153
Still Life with Tankards (Bodegón jarras). 1972.
Oil on canvas, 32 × 39³/₈ in. (81.2 × 100 cm).
Museo de Arte Moderno/I.N.B.A., Mexico City.

154
Dancers (Danzantes). 1972.
Oil on canvas, 53¹/₈ × 37³/₈ in. (135 × 95 cm).
Mark Schwarz Collection Quebec.

155
Image in a Looking-Glass (Imagen en un espejo).
1972.
Oil on canvas, 39³/₈ × 31¹/₂ in. (100 × 80 cm).
Kokusai Building Collection, Tokyo.

156
*Study in Blue and Brown (Estudio en azal
Y marrón).* 1973.
Oil on canvas 57¹/₈ × 42¹/₂ in. (145 × 108 cm).
Bernard Lewin Collection, Los Angeles, California.

157
Fish Vendors (Vendedores de pescado). 1972.
Oil on canvas, 38¹/₄ × 50³/₈ in. (97 × 128 cm).
Jacob B. Noble Collection, Roslyn, New York.

158
Torso in Green (Torso en verde). 1973.
Oil on canvas, 37³/₈ × 53¹/₈ in. (95 × 135 cm).
Lee Ault Collection, New York.

159
The Clock (El reloj). 1973.
Oil on canvas, 39³/₈ × 31¹/₂ in. (100 × 80 cm).
Armando Garza Sada Collection, Monterrey.

160
Pink and Blue Head (Cabeza rosa y azul). 1972.
Oil on canvas, 15 × 9⁷/₈ in. (38 × 25 cm).
Bernard Lewin Collection, Los Angeles, California.

161
Pink and Yellow Head (Cabeza rosa y amarilla).
1972.
Oil on canvas, 15 × 9⁷/₈ in. (38 × 25 cm).
Bernard Lewin Collection, Los Angeles, California.

162
Woman in Ecstasy (Mujer en éxtasis). 1973.
Oil on canvas, 51¹/₄ × 76³/₄ in. (130 × 195 cm).
Private collection.

163
Figure in Pink (Figura en rosa). 1974.
Oil on canvas, 29¹/₂ × 21⁵/₈ in. (75 × 55 cm).
Manuel de Muga Collection, Barcelona.

164
Character (Personaje). 1973.
Oil on canvas, 31¹/₂ × 49¹/₄ in. (80 × 125 cm).
Diego Sada Collection, Monterrey.

165
Children in Red (Niños en rojo). 1973.
Oil on canvas, 47¹/₄ × 57¹/₈ in. (120 × 145 cm).
Phoenix Art Museum, Phoenix, Arizona.

166
Woman (Mujer). 1973.
Oil on canvas, 19¹/₄ × 15³/₄ in. (49 × 40 cm).
Robert G. Rouckie Collection, Union City,
New Jersey.

167
Head (Cabeza). 1973.
Oil on canvas, 17³/₄ × 13³/₄ in. (45 × 35 cm).
J. H. Sherman Collection Baltimore Maryland.

168
Smiling Head (Cabeza que sonrie). 1973.
Oil on canvas, 14⁵/₈ × 14⁵/₈ in. (37 × 37 cm).
Bernard Lewin Collection, Los Angeles, California

169
Couple (Pareja). 1973.
Oil on canvas, 17⁷/₈ × 26 in. (45.5 × 66 cm).
Private collection, U.S.A.

170
Couple *(Pareja).* 1973.
Oil on canvas, 31¹/₂ × 39³/₈ in. (80 × 100 cm).
Harvey Amsterdam Collection, New *York.*

171
Man in White (Hombre en blanco). 1973.
Oil on canvas, 76³/₄ × 53¹/₈ in. (195 × 135 cm).
Márgara Garza Sada de Fernández Collection,
Monterrey.

172
Head in Grey (Cabeza en gris). 1973.
Oil on canvas, 39³/₈ × 31⁷/₈ in. (100 × 81 cm).
Museo de Arte Moderno/I.N.B.A., Mexico City.

173
Woman Behind Glass (Mujer detrás de un vidrio)
1973.
Oil on canvas, 43¹/₄ × 59 in. (110 × 150 cm).
Private collection Mexico.

174
The Leader (El líder). 1973.
Oil on canvas, 51¹/₄ × 38¹/₄ in. (130 × 97 cm).
Museo de Arte Moderno/I.N.B.A., Mexico City.

175
Memorial Bust (Busto conmemorativo). 1973.
Oil on canvas, 43¹/₄ × 59 in. (110 × 150 cm).
Gilberto Borja Navarrete, Mexico City.

176
Gymnasts in Pink (Gimnastas en rosa). 1974.
Oil on canvas, 59 × 51¹/₄ in. (150 × 130 cm).
Marcos Misha Collection, Mexico City.

177
Children in a Round (Ronda de niños). 1974.
Oil on canvas, 53¹/₈ × 76³/₄ in. (135 × 195 cm).
Mimi Indaco Collection, Mexico.

178
High-Voltage Pylon
(Torre de alta *tensión).* 1974.
Oil on canvas, 76³/₄ × 51¹/₄ in.
(195 × 130 cm).
Olga Tamayo Collection, Mexico City.

179
Construction (Construcción). 1974.
Oil on canvas 76¾ × 51¼ in. (195 × 130 cm).
Galerie de France Paris.

180
Blocked Road (Camino cerrado). 1974.
Oil on canvas, 27⅝ × 43¼ in. (70 × 110 cm).
Olga Tamayo Collection Mexico City.

181
The Comedians (Los comediantes). 1974.
Oil on canvas, 37⅜ × 51¾ in. (95 × 130 cm).
Armando Garza Sada Collection Monterrey.

182
Carnival (Carnavalesca). 1974.
Oil on canvas, 76¾ × 51¼ in. (195 × 130 cm).
Bernardo Garza Sada Collection Monterrey.

183
Character (Personaje). 1974.
Oil on canvas, 51¼ × 37⅜ in. (130 × 95 cm).
Private collection.

184
The Juggler (El juglar). 1974.
Oil on canvas, 45¼ × 55⅛ in. (115 × 140 cm).
Mary-Anne Martin Collection, New *York.*

185
Portrait of the Devil (Retrato del diablo). 1974.
Oil on canvas, 55⅛ × 45¼ in. (140 × 115 cm).
Víctor Bravo Ahuja Collection, Mexico City.

186
Blonde Woman (Mujer rubia). 1974.
Oil on canvas, 76¾ × 51¼ in. (195 × 130 cm).
Galerie de France, Paris.

187
The Indiscreet Window (La ventana indiscreta).
1974.
Oil on canvas, 76¾ × 51¼ in. (195 × 130 cm).
Galerie de France, Paris.

188
The Beach (La playa). 1974.
Oil on canvas, 43¼ × 49¼ in. (110 × 125 cm).
Márgara Garza Sada de Fernandez Collection Monterrey.

189
Arid Landscape (Paisaje árido). 1974.
Oil on canvas, 53⅛ × 63 in. (135 × 160 cm).
Armando Garza Sada Collection Monterrey.

190
Show Dog (Perro de exposición). 1974.
Oil on canvas, 53⅛ × 76¾ in. (135 × 195 cm).
Museo de Arte Moderno Caracas.

191
Head (Cabeza). 1974.
Oil on canvas, 18½ × 15 in. (47 × 38 cm).
Alinka Zabludowsky Collection, Mexico City.

192
Dialogues (Diálogos). 1974.
Oil on canvas, 53⅛ × 76¾ in. (135 × 195 cm).
Bernard Lewin Collection, Los Angeles, California.

193
Head in White (Cabeza en blanco). 1975.
Oil on canvas, 31½ × 39⅜ in. (80 × 100 cm).
Armando Garza Sada Collection Monterrey.

194
Figure in White (Figura en blanco). 1975.
Oil on canvas, 51¼ × 37⅜ in. (130 × 95 cm).
Jacobo Zabludowsky Collection, Mexico City.

195
Man with His Arms Raised (Hombre con brazos en alto). 1975.
Acrylic on canvas, 38¼ × 51¼ in. (97 × 130 cm).
Private collection, Mexico.

196
The Twins (Las gemelas). 1975.
Oil on canvas, 57⅛ × 43¼ in. (145 × 110 cm).
Silvia Ripstein Collection, New York.

197
The Shout (El grito). 1975.
Oil on canvas, 51¼ × 37⅜ in. (130 × 95 cm).
Jacobo Zabludowsky Collection, Mexico City.

198
Double Portrait (Doble retrato). 1975.
Acrylic on canvas, 33½ × 39⅜ in. (85 × 100 cm).
Gilberto Borja Collection, Mexico City.

199
Striped Figure (Figura rayada). 1975.
Oil on canvas, 51¼ × 38¼ in. (130 × 97 cm).
Museum of Modern Art, Tokyo.

200
Two figures (Dos figuras). 1975.
Acrylic on canvas, 51¼ × 38¼ in. (130 × 97 cm).
Private collection, Mexico.

201
Woman and Her Ghost (Mujer y su fantasma).
1975.
Oil on canvas, 68⅞ × 55⅛ in. (175 × 140 cm).
Private collection, Mexico City.

202
Character in Red (Personaje en rojo). 1975.
Acrylic on canvas, 51¼ × 38¼ in. (130 × 97 cm).
Private collection.

203
Dialogue (Diálogo). 1975.
Oil on canvas, 43¼ × 57⅜ in. (110 × 145 cm).
Jacobo Zabludowsky Collection, Mexico City.

204
Man in Red and Green (Hombre en rojo y verde,
1975.
Oil on canvas, 51¼ × 37⅜ in. (130 × 95 cm).
José Pintado Collection, Mexico City.

205
Man Beside a Wall (Hombre junto a un muro).
1975.
Oil on canvas, 37⅜ × 51¼ in. (95 × 130 cm).
Robert and Avy Miller Collection, Encino, California.

206
The Red Hand (La mano roja). 1975.
Acrylic on canvas, 37⅜ × 51¼ in. (95 × 130 cm).
Jacobo Zabludowsky Collection, Mexico City.

207
Man Close to the Window (Hombre cerca de la ventana). 1975.
Oil on canvas, 51¼ × 37⅜ in. (130 × 95 cm).
Neda Anhalt Collection, Mexico City.

208
The Green Door (La puerta verde). 1975.
Acrylic on canvas, 39⅜ × 59 in. (100 × 150 cm).
Jacobo Zabludowsky Collection, Mexico City.

209
Emergent Man (Hombre emergente). 1975.
Oil on canvas, 31½ × 39⅜ in. (80 × 100 cm).
Museo de Bellas Artes, Caracas.

210
Still Life (Bodegón). 1976.
Oil on canvas, 31⅞ × 39⅜ in. (81 × 100 cm).
Armando Garza Sada Collection, Monterrey.

211
Boy in Red (Niño en rojo). 1975.
Oil on canvas, 38¼ × 53⅛ in. (97 × 135 cm).
Private collection, U.S.A.

212
Monumental to an Unknown Hero (Monumento a un héroe desconocido). 1975.
Oil on canvas, 51¾ × 38¼ in. (130 × 97cm).
Private collection, Los Angeles, California.

213
Still Life (Bodegón). 1975.
Oil on canvas, 31⅞ × 39⅜ in. (81 × 100 cm).
Anna Bonomi Collection, Milan.

214
Landscape in Grey (Paisaje en gris). 1975.
Oil on canvas, 23⅝ × 33½ in. (60 × 85 cm).
Jacobo Zabludowsky Collection, Mexico City.

215
The Forgotten Clock (El reloj olvidado). 1975.
Acrylic on canvas, 38¼×51¼ in. (97×130 cm).
Olga Tamayo Collection, Mexico City.

216
Character in Green (Personaje en verde). 1975.
Oil on canvas, 39⅜×31½ in. (100×80 cm).
Neda Anhalt Collection, Mexico City.

217
Two Figures (Dos figuras). 1975.
Oil on canvas, 53⅛×76¾ in. (135×195 cm).
Anna Bonomi Collection, Milan.

218
Boy in Red (Niño en rojo). 1976.
Oil on canvas, 51¼×38¼ in. (130×97 cm).
Private collection, Mexico.

219
Still Life (Naturaleza muerta). 1976.
Oil on canvas, 31½×39⅜ in. (80×100 cm).
Arnaldo Pomodoro Collection, Milan.

220
Arrangement (Arreglo). 1976.
Oil on canvas, 51¼×38¼ in. (130×97 cm).
Private collection, New York.

221
Woman in White (Mujer en blanco). 1976.
Oil on canvas, 39⅜×31½ in. (100×80 cm).
Alberto Sánchez Palazuelos Collection .

222
Man in Red (Hombre en rojo). 1976.
Oil on canvas 51¼×38⅝ in. (130×98 cm).
Museo Rufino Tamayo/I.N.B.A., Mexico City.

223
Hippy Woman (Mujer hippy). 1976.
Oil on canvas, 51¼×38¼ in. (130×97 cm).
Private collection, Mexico.

224
Still Life with Fruit Bowl (Bodegón con frutero).
1976.
Oil on canvas, 38¼×51¾ in. (97×130 cm).
Rómulo Betancourt Collection, Caracas.

225
Man at the Window (Hombre en la ventana). 1976.
Oil on canvas, 31½×39⅜ in. (80×100 cm).
Private collection, Brazil.

226
Pile of Plates (Pila de platos). 1977.
Oil on canvas, 31⅞×39⅜ in. (81×100 cm).
Private collection, New York.

227
Man (Hombre). 1976.
Oil on canvas, 51¼×38¼ in. (130×97 cm).
Mauricio Berger Collection.

228
Nude in White (Desnudo en blanco). 1976.
Oil on canvas, 76¾×53⅛ in. (195×135 cm).
Museo Rufino Tamayo/I.N.B.A., Mexico City.

229
Empty Fruit Bowl (Frutero vacío). 1976.
Oil on canvas, 59×43½ in. (150×110.5 cm).
Galería Arvil, Mexico City.

230
Woman in a Cave (Mujer en una cueva). 1977.
Oil on canvas, 53⅛×39⅜ in. (135×100 cm).
Alinka Zabludowsky Collection, Mexico City.

231
Pregnant Woman (Mujer embarazada). 1976.
Oil on canvas, 39⅜×31⅞ in. (100×81 cm).
Lucha Villa Collection, Mexico City.

232
The Great Galaxy (La gran galaxia). 1978.
Oil on canvas, 38¼×54¼ in. (97×137.8 cm).
Museo Rufino Tamayo/I.N.B.A., Mexico City.

233
Aerial Space (Espacio aéreo). 1977.
Oil on canvas, 39⅜×31⅞ in. (100×81 cm).
Private collection, Mexico.

234
Dancer (Danzante). 1977.
Oil on canvas, 68½×54¾ in. (174×139 cm).
The Solomon R. Guggenheim Museum,
New York.

235
*Two Men in a Landscape (Dos hombres en un
paisaje)*. 1977.
Oil on canvas, 38×51½ in. (96.5×130.8 cm).
Private collection, Mexico.

236
*Man with His Hands Clasped (Hombre con las
manos cruzadas)*. 1978.
Oil on canvas, 53⅛×37⅜ in. (135×95 cm).
Mme Susan Lloyd Collection, Paris.

237
Waning Moon (Cuarto menguante). 1978.
Acrylic on canvas, 76¾×53⅛ in. (195×135 cm).
Privatecollection U.S.A.

238
*Man with Crossed Arms (Hombre con los brazos
cruzados)*. 1978.
Oil on canvas, 38¼×51¼ in. (97×130 cm).
Private collection, Mexico City.

239
*Two Figures on a Purple Background (Dos figuras
sobre fondo morado)*. 1978.
Oil on canvas, 53⅛×37⅜ in. (135×95 cm).
Gian Franco Arnoldi Collection.

240
Red Head (Cabeza roja). 1978.
Oil on canvas, 39⅜×31½ in. (100×80 cm).
Mme Susan Lloyd Collection, Paris.

241
Standing Woman (mujer de pie). 1978.
Oil on canvas, 59×43¼ in. (150×110 cm).
Private collection, Mexico.

242
*Figure in White and Yellow (Figura en blanco y
amarillo)*. 1978.
Oil on canvas, 53⅛×43¼ in. (135×110 cm).
Private collection, Mexico.

243
Man at the Door (Hombre a la puerta). 1978.
Oil on canvas, 43¼×53⅛ in. (110×135 cm).
Private collection, U.S.A.

244
Torso (Torso). 1978.
Oil on canvas, 31½×39⅜ in. (80×100 cm).
David Somerset Collection, London.

245
Ghost at the Door (Fantasma a la puenta). 1978.
Oil on canvas, 38¼×51¼ in. (97×130 cm).
Bernard Lewin Collection, Los Angeles, California.

246
Two Women (Dos mujeres). 1979.
37⅜×51¼ in. (95×130 cm).
Private collection, Caracas.

247
Woman Smiling (Mujer sonriente). 1979.
Oil on canvas, 51¼×37⅜ in. (130×95 cm).
Private collection, U.S.A.

248
Acrobat (Saltimbanqui). 1979.
Oil on canvas, 53⅛×37⅜ in. (135×95 cm).
Bernard Lewin Collection, Los Angeles, California.

249
Man (Hombre). 1979.
Acrylic on canvas, 51¼×37⅜ in. (130×95 cm).
Bernard Lewin Collection, Los Angeles, California.

250
Man (Personaje). 1979.
Acrylic on canvas, 76¾×51¼ in. (195×130 cm).
Mr and Mrs Stephen Jacobson Collection.

251
Man and His Ghost (Hombre y su fantasma). 1980.
Oil on canvas, 59×43¼ in. (150×110 cm).
Industrias Resistol Collection, Mexico.

252
Dancer (Danzante). 1980.
Acrylic on canvas, 51¼×37⅜ in. (130×95 cm).
Museo Rufino Tamayo/I.N.B.A., Mexico City.

253
The Man with the Sabre (El hombre del sable).
1980.
Acrylic on canvas, 51¼ × 37⅜ in. (130 × 95 cm).
Claude Terrain Collection, Mexico City.

254
Man (Hombre). 1979.
Acrylic on canvas, 51¼ × 37⅜ in. (130 × 95 cm).
Private collection.

255
Friends of the Birds (Amigas de los pájaros).
1980.
Oil on canvas, 51¼ × 37⅜ in. (130 × 95 cm).
Grupo Industrial Alfa Collection, Monterrey.

256
Shout (Grito). 1980.
Acrylic on canvas, 51¼ × 37⅜ in. (130 × 95 cm).

257
*Man Attacked by a Bird (Hombre atacado por un
pájaro).* 1980.
Acrylic on canvas, 51 × 38 in. (129.5 × 96.5 cm).
Esthela Santos Collection, Monterrey.

258
Men Walking (Hombres caminando). 1980.
Oil on canvas, 51 × 37 in. (129.5 × 94 cm).
Mr Tony Randall Collection, New York.

259
Boy with Cap (Niño con cachucha). 1980.
Oil on canvas, 39½ × 31⅜ in. (100.3 × 79.7 cm).

260
*Character in an Interior (Personaje en un
interior).* 1981.
Oil on canvas, 31½ × 49¼ in. (80 × 125 cm).
Marlborough Gallery, New York.

261
Man and Woman (Hombre y mujer). 1981.
Oil on canvas, 37⅜ × 53⅛ in. (95 × 135 cm).

262
*Three Characters Singing (Tres personajes
cantando).* 1981.
Oil on canvas, 37⅜ × 53⅛ in. (95 × 135 cm).
Private collection, Mexico.

263
Two Characters (Dos personajes). 1981.
Oil on canvas, 37⅜ × 53⅜ in. (95 × 135 cm).

264
Couple on the Terrace (Pareja en la terraza).
1981.
Oil on canvas, 51 × 71 in. (129.5 × 180.4 cm).
Latin American Masters Gallery, Beverly Hills,
California.

265
Man and Woman (Hombre y mujer). 1981.
Oil on canvas, 49⅛ × 70⅞ in. (124.8 × 180 cm).
Tate Gallery London.

266
Red Torso (Torso rojo). 1981.
Oil on canvas 70⅞ × 49¼ in. (180 × 125 cm).
Bernard Lewin Collection, Los Angeles, California.

267
Nude Man (Desnudo de hombre). 1982.
Oil on canvas, 51¼ × 37⅜ in. (130 × 95 cm).
Bernardo and Irma Zarkin Collection, Mexico City.

268
Forgotten Clock (Reloj olvidado). 1986.
Oil on canvas, 38¼ × 51¼ in. (97 × 130 cm).
Olga Tamayo Collection, Mexico City.

269
The Family (La familia). 1987.
Oil on canvas, 53⅛ × 76¾ in. (135 × 195 cm).
Olga Tamayo Collection, Mexico City.

270
Offering of Fruits (Ofrenda de frutas). 1987.
Oil on canvas, 55⅛ × 68⅞ in. (140 × 175 cm).
Private collection, Mexico City.

271
The Three Friends (Los tres amigos). 1987.
Oil on canvas, 43¼ × 59⅞ in. (110 × 152 cm).
Marlborough Gallery Collection, New York, N.Y.

272
Today (Hoy). 1988.
Oil on canvas, 51¼ × 76¾ in. (130 × 195 cm).
Olga Tamayo Collection, Mexico City.

273
Bathers in Cancún (Bañistas en Cancún). 1988.
Oil on canvas, 37⅜ × 51¼ in. (95 × 130 cm).
Private collection, Mexico City.

274
Hands Up (Manos arriba). 1989.
Oil on canvas, 37⅜ × 51¼ in. (95 × 130 cm).
Latin American Masters Collection, Los Angeles,
California.

275
The Rock-and-Roll Dancer (El rockanrolero). 1989.
Oil on canvas, 71¼ × 49 in. (181 × 124.5 cm).
Olga Tamayo Collection, Mexico City.

276
Character Winking (Personaje guiñando un ojo).
1989.
Oil on canvas, 51¼ × 37⅜ in. (130 × 95 cm).
Ingeniero Gilberto Borja Navarrete Collection,
Mexico City.

277
*Character in an Interior (Personaje en un
interior).* 1989.
Oil on canvas, 37⅜ × 51¼ in. (95 × 130 cm).
Private collection, Mexico City.

278
Picasso Naked (Picasso al desnudo). 1989.
Oil on canvas, 51¼ × 37⅝ in. (130 × 95.5 cm).
Olga Tamayo Collection, Mexico City.

279
Man with a Flower (Hombre con flor). 1989.
Oil on canvas, 33⅞ × 26⅜ in. (86 × 67 cm).
Olga Tamayo Collection, Mexico City.

280
The Vase with Flowers (El vaso con flores).
1990.
Oil on canvas, 51¼ × 37⅜ in. (130 × 95 cm).
Marlborough Gallery, New York, N.Y.

281
*The Boy with the Bass Viol (El muchacho del
violón).* 1990.
Oil on canvas, 51¼ × 37¾ in. (130 × 96 cm).
Private collection Mexico City.

COLLECTIONS

Pictures by Tamayo are to be found in numerous private collections and in a great number of museums.

BELGIUM

Musées Royaux des Beaux-Arts, Brussels.

BRAZIL

Museu de Arte Moderna, Rio de Janeiro.

U.S.A

Albright-Knox Art Gallery, Buffalo.
Arizona State University Art Collections, Arizona.
Art Institute of Chicago, Chicago.
Brooklyn Museum, New York.
Cincinnati Art Museum, Cincinnati.
Cleveland Museum of Art, Cleveland.
Dallas Museum of Fine Arts, Dallas.
Fogg Art Museum, Harvard University, Cambridge.
Hirshhorn Museum and Sculpture Garden, Smithsonian Institution, Washington.
Humanities Research Center, University of Texas, Austin.
Krannert Art Museum, University of Illinois, Urbana-Champaign.
Los Angeles County Museum of Art, Los Angeles.
Milwaukee Art Center, Milwaukee.
Minneapolis Institute of Art, Minneapolis.
Museum of Art, Carnegie Institute, New York.
Museum of Art, Rhode Island School of Design, Providence.
Museum of Fine Arts, Houston.
Museum of Modern Art, Houston.
Museum of Modern Art, New York.
National Museum, Phoenix.
National Museum, St. Louis.
Philadelphia Museum of Art, Philadelphia.
Phillips Collection, Washington, D.C.
Phoenix Art Museum, Phoenix.
New York Public Library, New York.
San Francisco Museum of Art, San Francisco.
Smith College Museum of Art, Northampton, Massachusetts.
Solomon R. Guggenheim Museum, New York.
St. Louis Art Museum, St. Louis.
University of Louisville Allen R. Hite Art Institute, Kentucky.
University of Oregon, Oregon.
Washington University, St. Louis.
Washington University, St. Louis.
Wichita Art Museum, Wichita, Kansas.
Yale University Art Gallery, New Haven, Connecticut.

FRANCE

Musée National d'Art Moderne, Centre d'Art et de Culture Georges Pompidou, Paris.
UNESCO, Mural for Conference Room, Paris.

ENGLAND

Tate Gallery, London.

ISRAEL

Museum of Fine Arts, Jerusalem

ITALY

Galleria Nazionale d'Arte Moderna, Rome.
Musei Vaticani, Ciudad del Vaticano, Rome.

JAPAN

Museum of Modern Arts, Tokyo.

MEXICO

Museo del Palacio de Bellas Artes, Mexico City.
Museo de Arte Moderno, Mexico City.
Museo de Arte Contemporáneo Internacional Rufino Tamayo, Mexico City.
Museo de Monterrey, Monterrey, N.L.
Museo Nacional de Arte, Mexico City.

NORWAY

Museum Kunstnerns Hus, Oslo.
Nasjonalgalleriet, Oslo.

PUERTO RICO

Universidad de Puerto Rico, Río Piedras Campus.

VENEZUELA

Museo de Arte Moderno, Caracas.
Museo de Bellas Artes, Caracas.